WHEN I GROW UP

THE LOST AUTOBIOGRAPHIES OF SIX YIDDISH TEENAGERS

KEN KRIMSTEIN

BLOOMSBURY PUBLISHING

NEW YORK · LONDON · OXFORD · NEW DELHI · SYDNEY

BLOOMSBURY PUBLISHING
BLOOMSBURY PUBLISHING Inc.
1385 Broadway, New York, NY 10018, USA

BLOOMSBURY, BLOOMSBURY PUBLISHING, and the Diana logo are trademarks of
Bloomsbury Publishing Plc

First published in the United States 2021

Copyright © Ken Krimstein 2021

ISBN: HB: 978-1-63557-370-1; eBook: 978-1-63557-371-8

Library of Congress Cataloging-in-Publication Data is available

2 4 6 8 10 9 7 5 3 1

Printed and bound at Mohn Media Mohndruck GmbH, Germany

To find out more about our authors and books visit www.bloomsbury.com
and sign up for our newsletters.

Bloomsbury books may be purchased for business or promotional use. For
information on bulk purchases please contact Macmillan Corporate and
Premium Sales Department at specialmarkets@macmillan.com.

To these six

"Yiddishuania." The largest, most concentrated Jewish population the world has ever seen, with almost nine million people—poets, mystics, criminals, scientists, musicians, taxi drivers, firemen, pork-eaters, and, yes, even cartoonists—and with Vilna as its uncrowned capital.

CONTENTS

Preface: Crossing the Abyss

In the late summer of 2018 I held a miracle in my hands.

A student notebook. Its paper was unblemished and the writing, though indecipherable to me, was inked as crisply as if it had been written that afternoon. Except that it hadn't. The pages I'd flown halfway around the world to see had been jotted down more than eighty years earlier. In fact, the only evidence of the notebook's age, and its journey of being hidden twice, lost once, and finally unearthed just a year before I came across it, were three rusty shards that had once been staples, bloodred splinters ever so slightly staining irregular halos.

"Question," I said to the archivist at the Martynas Mažvydas National Library of Lithuania, "how many people have flipped through this notebook since 1939?"

"Two," she said. "You. And me."

Catching my breath, I turned another page.

THE BEFORE...

For as long as there have been Jews, there has been "the Jewish Question." More than just an "issue" for anti-Semites, for five thousand years or so it was THE question Jews

asked themselves: "How can one live as a Jew?" And answered: "Es iz shver tsu zeyn a yid"—the Yiddish trope "It's hard to be a Jew."

There was, however, a brief moment in the early twentieth century when, taking advantage of the nine million residents of Yiddishuania as well as the most recent advances in social science and psychology, linguist Max Weinreich* and a handful of writers, poets, artists, and Yiddish scholars at the Yidisher Visnshaftlekher Institut (YIVO), Yiddishuania's de facto university without walls (only fitting for its nation without borders), set out to answer that sticky question once and for all. And they set out to do it in their

* The person who famously quipped "A language is a dialect with an army and navy."

own particular YIVO fashion, combining rigorous science with daring improvisation. So in 1932, YIVO's Division of Youth Research, its Jugendforschung, birthed the audacious idea of

having Jewish youth lead the way. In a bold demonstration of their faith in the future, YIVO chose to privilege Yiddish thirteen-to-twenty-one-year-olds with defining a NEW kind of Jewish world, one that would

be both fully modern and fully Jewish.

The plan? An ethnographic study in the guise of a meagerly funded autobiography contest. The grand prize: 150 zlotys* for the best entry. Meaning the most TRUTHFUL entry. (Because what good would the autobiographies be if in the stories the "youth" submitted, they didn't spill the beans on what was really going on—not just the truth,

but even more to the point, their unvarnished version of the truth as they lived it?)

* Roughly a thousand U.S. dollars in 2021 money.

No topics were off limits— the more daring the better. The rules encouraged candor: "Do not think that only an individual with extraordinary experiences can enter, do not think that little things are unimportant, and above all, do not make your autobiographies 'more interesting' by inventing incidents or using 'flowery language.'" They even suggested some topics for the teens to cover:

YOU AND YOUR FAMILY, THE WAR YEARS, TEACHERS, SCHOOLS, BOYFRIENDS, GIRLFRIENDS, YOUTH ORGANIZATIONS, POLITICAL PARTY AFFILIATIONS AND WHAT THEY GAVE YOU, HOW YOU CAME TO YOUR OCCUPATION OR HOW YOU ARE PLANNING TO COME TO YOUR OCCUPATION, WHAT EVENTS IN YOUR LIFE MADE THE GREATEST IMPRESSION ON YOU.

But the real stroke of genius was that each entry to the competition would be ANONYMOUS! YIVO's social scientists understood teens well enough to know that nobody would write the whole truth about their parents if their parents would be able to read what they'd written. So they devised an elaborate procedure of coded entry, an arcanely developed systematization of addresses ensuring that the "winner" would get his or her booty without revealing a name.

Throughout the 1930s, more than seven hundred entries rolled in from all corners of Yiddishuania. Each was meticulously logged, read, studied, and judged by the YIVO staff in Vilna. And what was the big day that the Grand Prize was to be awarded? September 1, 1939. The very day the Nazis invaded Poland and the Second World War commenced. Needless to say, the awards were canceled due to more pressing matters.

Like survival.

But here the story really just gets started. On June 24 of 1941, the moment the Nazis conquered Vilna, they raced to the library of YIVO and pirated away as much of its contents as they could carry to form the cornerstone of Hitler's Institut zur Erforschung der Judenfrage.*

And who did the Nazis enlist (at the end of a gun barrel) to sort and select these Jewish treasures? The very librarians

* The Institute for Study of the Jewish Question, founded by the Nazis in 1939, opened in Frankfurt in 1941 and run by Johannes Pohl.

who had collected them in the first place. But, well aware of the irreplaceable nature of everything in the YIVO archives—the autobiographies included—the poets, artists, and scholar slave laborers risked their lives to smuggle what they could away from the pseudohistorians of the Gestapo, hiding it in caches throughout the Vilna Ghetto. These forty brave souls came to be known as The Paper Brigade (only eight of them survived the war).

The next chapter in the odyssey of the autobiographies begins on July 13, 1944, when

the Soviets reconquered Vilna from the Nazis. The euphoric survivors of the Paper Brigade wasted no time in unearthing their treasures (including hundreds of the autobiographies) and establishing the Vilna Jewish Museum amidst the smoldering remains of the city. What's more, with diplomatic deference, in an effort to placate Joseph Stalin, dictator of Soviet Russia, they even dedicated the opening exhibition to him.

Nevertheless, just five years later, in 1949, after the newly created State of Israel sided with the West instead of

Stalin, the pipe-smoking, bushy-mustachioed dictator ordered the entire contents of the museum pulped in retaliation.

Now, however, another hero stood up, in the unlikely guise of a stoic non-Jewish Lithuanian librarian and Communist Party official named Antanas Ulpis. At risk of life and limb (again!), Ulpis cadged the YIVO trove and ferreted the valuable documents away from the KGB, stashing them and more than 180,000 pages of other Yiddish documents in the silent organ pipes and overturned confessionals of St. George's Church, a "decommissioned" cathedral in central Vilna (by then known as Vilnius). Here these notebooks slept, lost, forgotten, invisible for more than seventy years, until the fall of 2017, when, while doing a final clean out of the church, workers stumbled across them, including the pages I'd flown to Vilnius to see and would be holding in my hands less than a year later.

What follows are a handful of those stories. Unvarnished lives told by anonymous Yiddishuanian teens looking ahead to their future, a future we now know nobody could have imagined, and nobody can still quite comprehend: the complete and utter annihilation of Yiddishuania, its towns, its

people without names to once again speak their words, the words of youth, to fill that void.

What happened to the authors of these narratives? Sadly, with one exception (whose story is among those that follow), we don't know for sure. But one thing we do know is that these were vibrant, complicated, candid, self-aware teenagers; unapologetic, ornery, and know-it-all like all teenagers everywhere; resolute young men and young women with a story to tell and a question to answer. Here are six of them.

cities, its stories, its treasures, its language, its people.

A hole in history.

By harnessing their words, hopes, dreams, and actions, as well as imagery from the times and places they inhabited, I've enlisted the form of the nonfiction graphic narrative in an attempt to allow these

10

Vilnius, Lithuania, September 2018

11

THE EIGHTH DAUGHTER
19-year-old girl

15/8 1932

* I. L. Peretz (1852–1915). One of the "big three" of Yiddish literature; the progressive, modernist, yet strangely-anchored-in-the-world-of-Yiddish-folklore-and-fables one.

AS WAS THE CUSTOM BACK THEN, MY GREAT-GRANDMOTHER ON MY MOTHER'S SIDE WAS MARRIED AT THE AGE OF TWELVE.

ONE DAY, WHEN SHE WAS TAKING CARE OF A COW, SHE FELL ASLEEP, AND IT GOT INTO THE BARLEY AND ATE IT ALL UP.

MUNCH MUNCH

ZZZZZ

WHEN MY GREAT-GREAT-GRANDFATHER FOUND OUT, HE YELLED AT HER...

...RIGHT IN FRONT OF HER HUSBAND!!!

AS FOR ME, MY FATHER OWNS A KOSHER BUTCHER SHOP.

SKUBELK

APTHEK

BUT EVEN THOUGH HE'S JUST A SHOKHET,*

THAT DIDN'T KEEP HIM FROM READING YIDDISH LITERATURE.

LOOK, I KNOW WHAT MENDL SFORIM** SAYS ABOUT KOSHER MEAT IN HIS STORIES, BUT MY PRICES ARE FAIR AND SQUARE.

AND THAT PERETZ, HE'S A GREAT WRITER, A REAL GENIUS, BUT I DON'T TELL HIM HOW TO WRITE HIS STORIES...

HE SHOULD TELL ME HOW TO GEHAKHT*** MY CHICKENS?

* Kosher butcher

** Mendele Mocher Sforim (1836–1917). Another one of the "big three" of Yiddish writing, often referred to by his student and protege Sholem Aleichem, as the father—well, the grandfather of it all. Realist/fabulist, Sforim was writing fierce comic parables during the time of the American Civil War that rival anything Kafka would come up with seventy years later. His nom de plume means "Mendl the Bookseller."

*** Chop

FOR THE WHOLE TWENTY-THREE YEARS THAT HE WORKED, MY FATHER NEVER QUARRELED WITH ANYONE, AND NEVER TOOK SIDES IN ANY DISPUTES.

HE'S A MENSCH* WITH A VERY SHARP KNIFE.

PUT A FINGER ON THE SCALE? HE'D AS SOON CUT IT OFF!

IT'S CUSTOM FOR THE SHOKHET TO KEEP THE SPLEEN, BUT ONE WINTER, WHEN MY HUSBAND WAS DOWN WITH PNEUMONIA...

HE GAVE US THE SPLEEN—FREE!

HEY, IF YOU'VE GOT TO BE BORN A CHICKEN, YOU COULD DO A LOT WORSE THAN WINDING UP AT HIS SHOP.

* A righteous person, a good dude, someone who's solid.

WHEN I WAS SIX, ONE OF MY SISTERS FELL ILL AND DIED.

MY FATHER SOOTHED ME.

I SAW HE WAS ALSO CRYING.

DADDY, GROWN-UPS CAN CRY TOO?

DON'T CRY.

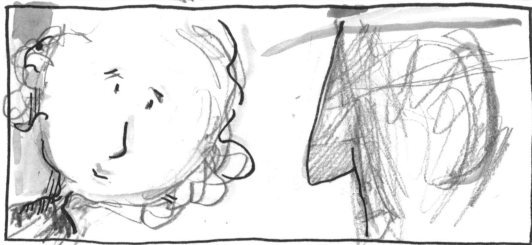

HE MADE ME FEEL BETTER.

SO MUCH THAT RIGHT AFTER THE BURIAL, I WENT OUT TO PLAY.

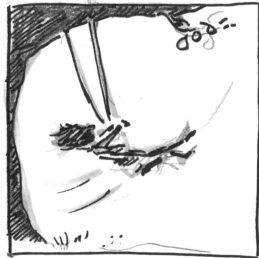

BUT OTHER THINGS AT HOME WEREN'T ALWAYS SO SMOOTH.

MY OLDEST SISTER DIDN'T GET ALONG WITH MY MOTHER.

AND MOTHER DIDN'T LIKE HER BACK.

MY OTHER SIX SISTERS...

MINE!

MINE!

WERE BUSY DOING WHAT OTHER SISTERS DO.

CUTE.

UGLY.

LIAR.

BITCH.

GET OUT OF THE BATHROOM ALREADY!

HUH?

FACE IT, NO AMOUNT OF MAKEUP WILL HELP.

IT'S JUST A DATE.

AS FOR ME, I THREW MYSELF INTO SCHOOL—MY PARADISE.

I STARTED READING BOOKS.

AND I COULDN'T STOP.

I WAS FORBIDDEN TO READ THINGS THAT WERE THOUGHT TO BE INAPPROPRIATE FOR ME.

FREUD

DOSTOEVSKY

FLAUBERT

WHICH ONLY MADE ME WANT TO READ THEM MORE.

ד' ברודער קאראמאזאוו *

ד' צוקונפֿט פֿון אַ יווג **

מאדאם באָוואַ ***

AT FIRST I WOULD ONLY ABSORB THE STORY, I WOULDN'T GET THAT DEEP INTO THEM.

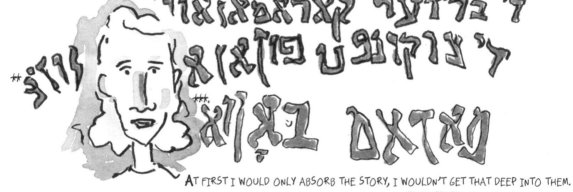

BUT LISTENING TO EVERYONE ELSE AT HOME DISSECT A BOOK, I BEGAN TO UNDERSTAND THAT IN EVERY BOOK, ONE MUST LOOK TO FIND SOMETHING MORE. I SOAKED UP EVERY WORD.

SOCIALIST!

NEOMODERNIST.

NATURALISM IS A LIE.

IRONIC, CYNICAL COMMUNISM.

RELAX, WHAT THE AUTHOR'S TRYING TO SAY IS THAT SYMBOLS ARE REAL.

* *The Brothers Karamazov* (Dostoevsky), translated into Yiddish in 1923.
** *The Future of an Illusion* (Freud), translated into Yiddish in 1932.
*** *Madame Bovary* (Flaubert), translated into Yiddish in 1928.

THEN I STARTED TO WRITE...

MY OWN STORIES.

MY EDITOR WAS THE SISTER TWO OLDER THAN ME.

I DON'T BELIEVE THIS SCENE.

OY VEY!

MUCH BETTER—NOW YOU'RE COOKING WITH GAS!

THIS IS GOOD.

VERY.

WHEN SHE PRAISED SOMETHING I WROTE, I WOULD BE HAPPY.

WHICH GOT ME THINKING.

27

At this point, I should add that from childhood on, I had an inborn characteristic: sincerity mixed with a childish naivety.

Which means I didn't hold back anything, but expressed everything.

AND SO, ONE MORNING AFTER MY "EDITOR" PRAISED MY LATEST LITERARY EFFORT...

30

* Story by Peretz written in 1906, translated as "Bontsha the Silent," wherein a common man argues for the sanctity of his soul and his life in a heavenly tribunal with very uncertain and unsettling results.

* A highly controversial and unusual stance, there has been a lively debate (mostly among men) going on for a couple of thousand years whether it is even kosher for a woman to be a kosher butcher.

BUT EVERY NIGHT WHEN PAPA CAME HOME FROM WORK, HE'D HAVE SUCH TERRIBLE ANGINA PAINS IN HIS HEART THAT MY MOTHER, MY GRANDMOTHER, MYSELF, AND ALL MY SISTERS WOULD CRY.

IT'S NOTHING.

...OY.

AND THEN, ONE WINTER MORNING...

MY FATHER DIED.

AT FIRST, I DIDN'T REALIZE WHAT HAD HAPPENED.

I FELT IT MORE THAN I UNDERSTOOD IT.

BUT WHEN WE RIPPED OUR CLOTHES IN MOURNING,* I UNDERSTOOD THAT MY FATHER HAD LEFT US FOREVER. SOMETHING IN ME TORE AND SEETHED. I FELT ORPHANED. I FELT EMPTY, AS IF PART OF ME HAD BEEN TAKEN AWAY.

* The ritual is called "kriah," where everyone in the family gets to tear their clothes as a tangible sign of grief.

AS WAS THE CUSTOM, THE FUNERAL WAS ARRANGED FOR THE NEXT DAY.
SINCE MY FATHER WAS SUCH A BIG MACHER* THE CHEVRA KADISHA**
TOOK CARE OF EVERYTHING. HE WAS DRAPED IN HIS SHROUD, AND AS WE
PROCEEDED THROUGH TOWN, EVEN THE POLISH POLICE STOPPED TRAFFIC
AND EVERYONE PAUSED THE REQUIRED FIVE SECONDS. I COULDN'T STOP
HOPING THAT MY FATHER MANAGED TO REMEMBER HIS NAME WHEN THE
ANGEL OF DEATH ASKED HIM.***

* Slightly smaller cheese than the gabbai, but not much.
** The Burial Society, kind of a social "A"-list for the deceased, presided over by the gabbai, aka "the big cheese."
*** According to Jewish folklore, the moment the angel of death comes, he or she asks your name. If you don't get it right, you're doomed for
eternity. If you sort of get it right, you suffer "Hibbut ha-Kever," thrashing pains in the grave. To aid memory for just this occasion, special books were
sold with passages from the psalms organized to spur memory; passages that started with the first letter of their name and ended with the last.

* The Jewish Sabbath
** Synagogue
*** Praying with lots of fervor, often involving rocking back and forth and mumbling very very fast.

37

KAYZER, THE SHAMUS,* RACED UPSTAIRS TO THE WOMEN'S BALCONY.

* The "boss" of the synagogue—a combination know-it-all, fixer, enforcer, fundraiser, and administrator.

AT THAT MOMENT, PERHAPS FOR THE FIRST TIME, I BEGAN **NOT** TO UNDERSTAND GOD.

MY KADDISH WAS FERVENT, I BELIEVED THAT EVERYTHING PEOPLE DO IS BY GOD'S WILL.

WHY WOULDN'T THE SHAMUS LET ME STAND FOR THE AMIDAH*?

STILL ALL THESE YEARS LATER, MY HEART YEARNS

* The central, extremely long prayers and blessings uttered first in silence and then repeated aloud, and always said standing whether it's private or public.

* Oyfern — "CLOSED" — AKA "THAT'S ALL SHE WROTE."

THE LETTER-WRITER
20-year-old boy

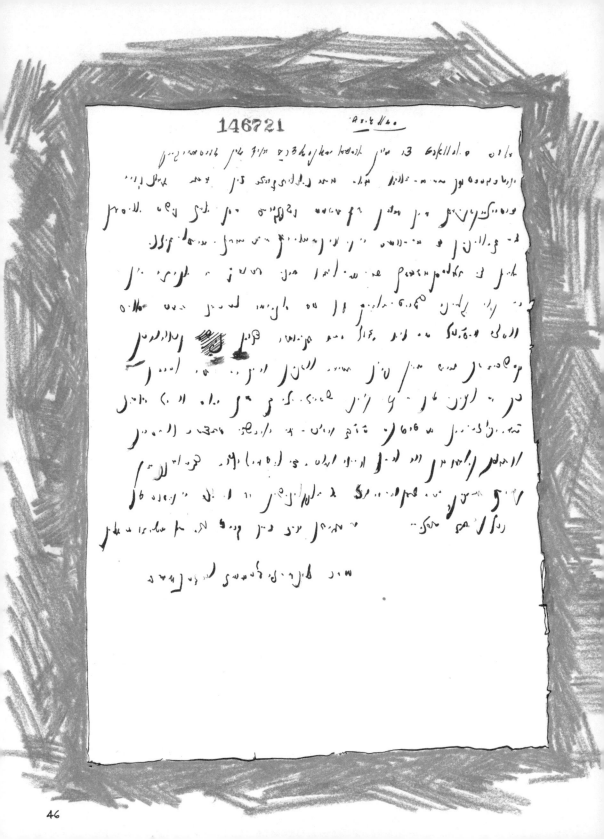

MY FAMILY WAS WELL-OFF, WE WERE IN THE WHEAT BUSINESS.

UNCLE SHMERKE LEAVES FOR AMERIKA!

SIGNING THE BIG LOAN

ST. MORITZ

* *Der Moment*, one of the two most important Yiddish daily newspapers published out of Warsaw from 1905 until two weeks before WWII started in 1939.
** *Haynt*, meaning "Today," the other big Yiddish daily, also published in Warsaw from 1906 to 1939; by 1913 its circulation was 150,000 copies a day and it kept going up from there, until it didn't.

49

WHEN MY FATHER HAD OTHER BUSINESSMEN OVER, I WOULD HOLD FORTH AND SURPRISE THEM BY EXPRESSING MY VARIOUS POLITICAL OPINIONS.

* Yiddish quip that became popular in the early twentieth century speaking to the defiance of some traditional Jews (with their beards and caftans) toward their more "Western-looking," clean-shaven fellow (or not-so-fellow?) co-religionists.

FROM READING ALL THOSE NEWSPAPERS, I SOON REALIZED THAT WE JEWISH KIDS HAD TO ORGANIZE!

...AND THAT'S WHY WE MUST MUST MUST FORM A BRANCH OF HEKHALUTZ HAMERKAZ!*

AND WE MUST DO IT TONIGHT. LET'S ALL MEET IN THE PINE FOREST CLEARING.

I'LL TAKE CARE OF EVERYTHING ELSE.

AND FOR THE FIRST TIME, THE WOODS AROUND ROGÓW** RESOUNDED WITH ZIONIST HYMNS.

* Zionist youth group so intent on defending themselves that they built practice collective farms in Eastern Europe so they could hit the Middle Eastern ground running.
** Now known as Raguva, Lithuania.

FOR MY BAR MITZVAH MY PARENTS INVITED EVERYONE IN TOWN.

EVEN MY COUSIN RACHEL CAME ALL THE WAY FROM AMERICA.

RACHEL!

LOOKIT!

ALL THE HOTTEST NEW SIDES* FROM THE COMMODORE MUSIC SHOP.**

IN THE MORNING THERE WAS A BIG PARTY FOR ALL THE ADULTS.

TODAY I AM A FOUNTAIN PEN!***

* Recorded hit song.
** Music shop founded in 1928 by Billy Crystal's uncle Milt Gabler.
*** Traditional bar mitzvah boy quip in response to the dozens of identical gifts from Sheaffer, Parker, and Waterman.

AND AT NIGHT, AN EVEN BIGGER PARTY FOR ALL MY FRIENDS.

WE PUT ON THE RECORD PLAYER AND DANCED 'TIL MIDNIGHT.

BUT THE JOY WAS SHORT-LIVED—

EVEN THOUGH I'D ACED MY EXAMS,
MY STUDIES WERE SOON TO BE OVER BECAUSE I WAS **JEWISH**.

MY MATH TEACHER OFFERED TO HELP, BUT SAID HE COULDN'T DO ANYTHING BECAUSE
"IT WAS IMPOSSIBLE."

I FELT THAT IT WAS AS IF ON A BEAUTIFUL SUMMER'S DAY A WIND BLEW...

...AND RAIN FELL AND BLOTTED OUT THE SUN AND DESTROYED THE BEAUTY OF EVERYTHING AROUND.

I MADE A VOW.

I'M QUITTING SCHOOL FOR GOOD.

A MONTH WENT BY, AND A YEAR.

I THOUGHT A LOT ABOUT WHO MIGHT BE ABLE TO HELP ME.

AND THEN, I ACTED.

I'LL START WRITING LETTERS!

genius!

MY FIRST LETTER WAS TO MEIR DIZENGOFF,** MAYOR OF TEL AVIV.

* Extreme audacity, like the boy who murdered his parents and plead for leniency in court because he was an "orphan."

** Meir Dizengoff (1861–1936). Russian-born engineer, soldier, freedom fighter, and the first mayor of Tel Aviv, a position he held until his death. Early in his career, he was an outspoken opponent of Theodor Herzl's idea of establishing the State of Israel in what is now Uganda.

I HAD STRAIGHT A'S IN SCHOOL...

...MY GIRLFRIEND WAS FORCED TO LEAVE ME, JUST LIKE THAT...

MY SOLE SOLACE IS SMOKING CIGARETTES AND READING THE NEWSPAPERS...

I RESOLVED TO QUIT SCHOOL FOR GOOD.

SHOULD I CONTINUE?

PLEASE.

ONLY IN THE FIELDS OF ZION CAN I ASSUAGE MY SADNESS.

RIFKA, TAKE A LETTER.

MY DEAR BOY, YOUR LETTER HAS MOVED ME GREATLY.

BUT, REGRETTABLY, DESPITE THAT, I AM SORRY TO REPORT THAT I DO NOT HAVE THE POWER TO GRANT YOU A CERTIFICATE.

MR. MAYOR, TELL HIM TO TRY THE JEWISH AGENCY.

SO, IT IS MY SUGGESTION THAT YOU TRY...

PLEASE, RIFKA, YOU JUST FINISH IT.

IT WAS AS IF A MYSTERIOUS HAND DROVE ME.

* Yiddish for "You have got to be kidding me!" The old question as a statement routine.

61

HOW MANY STAMPS FOR WASHINGTON, D.C., AMERICA?

PAVEL, COME HERE—GET A LOAD OF THIS ONE.

HOW MANY STAMPS FOR WASHINGTON, D.C.? WHO DOES HE THINK HE'S WRITING TO—THE PRESIDENT OF THE UNITED STATES?

YES.

THAT'S RIGHT. THIS TIME I BEGAN SEEKING HELP FROM NONE OTHER THAN FRANKLIN DELANO ROOSEVELT, THIRTY-SECOND PRESIDENT OF THE UNITED STATES.*

I'VE ALWAYS WANTED TO VISIT THE STATES.

ME TOO.

WHEN FDR WAS REELECTED I WROTE TO CONGRATULATE HIM AND, OF COURSE, AT THE SAME TIME TO USE THE OPPORTUNITY TO DESCRIBE MY SITUATION TO HIM.

* Also known as FDR, reelected THREE times (causing a change in the constitution), he served from 1933 to his death in 1945.

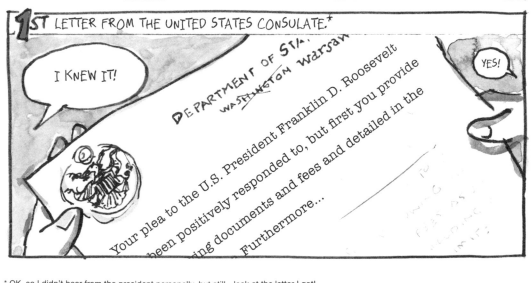

* OK, so I didn't hear from the president personally, but still—look at the letter I got!

IT TOOK ME SIX MONTHS TO GET ALL MY DOCUMENTS AND ALL THE MONEY THEY NEEDED FOR MY APPLICATION, BUT I DID IT.

AND THIS ONE, AND THIS, AND THIS, AND THIS...

2ND LETTER FROM THE UNITED STATES CONSULATE—THIS CAME BACK FAST, A GOOD SIGN.

DO YOU HAVE ANY FAMILY RESIDING IN THE UNITED STATES OF AMERICA?

THAT ONE WAS EASY.

OF COURSE HE DOES! ME! HIS UNCLE SHMERKE.

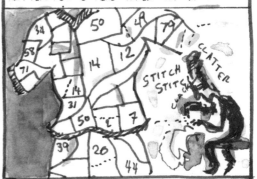

WHILE I WAS WAITING FOR MY PASSPORT TO ARRIVE, I DIDN'T JUST SIT AROUND DOING NOTHING. I TOOK UP LEARNING HOW TO TAILOR LADIES' GARMENTS.

STITCH STITCH CLATTER

I DIDN'T WANT TO BE A BURDEN TO ANYONE WHEN I ARRIVED IN NYC.

OUCH!

NO WORRIES.

I'M GOOD.

IT'LL HEAL

IN ADDITION WE STILL REQUIRE WRITTEN CONFIRMATION THAT SAID UNCLE WILL SPONSOR YOU AS WELL AS A STATEMENT QUALIFYING HIS ASSETS AND EARNINGS ALONG WITH HIS PERMANENT ADDRESS.
THANK YOU.

UNCLE SHMERKE GOT RIGHT BACK TO ME.

NO PROBLEMO!

4TH LETTER FROM U.S. CONSULATE.

PLEASE CLARIFY, SAID "UNCLE" MUST STATE THE UTTER DESPERATION OF YOUR SITUATION IN ADDITION TO SENDING ALONG HIS LATEST FOUR TAX RETURNS.
THANK YOU.

THIS TIME, TWO MONTHS PASSED BEFORE I RECEIVED A LETTER FROM UNCLE SHMERKE SAYING THAT HE WAS UNFORTUNATELY UNABLE TO PROVIDE HIS TAX RETURNS—BECAUSE HE PAID NO TAXES.

IT'S STRICTLY A CASH BUSINESS.

HARD THOUGH THIS WAS FOR ME TO SWALLOW, THE MYSTERIOUS FORCE CONTINUED TO SPUR ME ON. I HAD TO KEEP TRYING. SO I DECIDED TO WRITE TO ABRAHAM CAHAN,* EDITOR IN CHIEF OF THE AMERICAN EDITION OF THE YIDDISH **FORVERTS.**##

I TOLD HIM ABOUT MY SITUATION, AND ABOUT MY LETTER TO FDR.

NOW, THIS IS A REAL HERO.

TWO MONTHS LATER, I GOT A RESPONSE, BUT NOT FROM CAHAN. ONCE AGAIN I HEARD FROM UNCLE SHMERKE.

BUBALA! CAHAN RAN YOUR LETTER ON THE COVER OF **THE FORVERTS!**

ALONG WITH AN APPEAL TO SPONSOR YOU AND YOUR FAMILY!!!

* Abraham "Abe" Cahan (1860–1951). Russian-born American socialist newspaper editor. Trained to be a rabbi, he fled pogroms in 1882 all the way to Manhattan, where he ran *The Forverts* (*The Forward*), the world's largest Yiddish daily until his death. It was even printed in Poland, making it possibly the world's first global paper.
** Daily circulation of 275,000.

SO FAR MY
HOPES HAVE
NOT BEEN
FULFILLED.

BUT I KEEP
HOPING.

SIGNED,
ANONYMOUS BOY
ROGOW
APRIL 26,
1939

THE FOLK SINGER

19-year-old girl

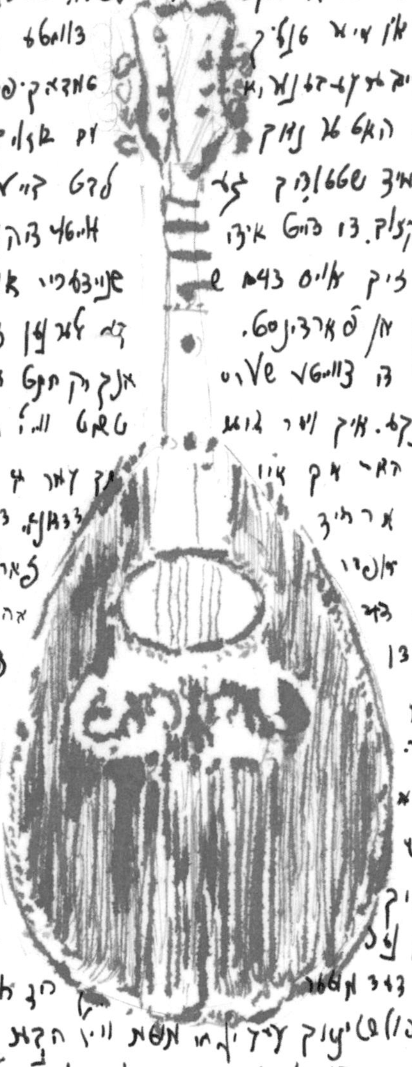

MY DAD KNEW EVERYTHING ABOUT EVERYTHING ON THE RADIO.

THAT'S HEIFETZ* PLAYING THE BRAHMS D MAJOR CONCERTO.

YOU'RE NOT HEARING HIS MUSIC...

YOU'RE HEARING HIS SOUL.

I STARTED PLAYING MANDOLIN AT A VERY YOUNG AGE. I WANTED TO GO TO THE MUSIC CONSERVATORY IN VILNA LIKE HEIFETZ. BUT, AS I WILL TELL, THE THREAD OF MY EARLY PASSION WAS SEVERED AND I WAS UNABLE TO FULFILL WHAT MIGHT HAVE BEEN.

AND ANYWAY, THEY DON'T TEACH MANDOLIN AT THE CONSERVATORY.

* Jascha Heifetz (1901–1987). Jewish musician, born in Vilna and considered the greatest violinist of all time.

 THE CHANGE STARTED WHEN ONE DAY, MY FATHER, WHO HAD BEEN A DEVOTED FAMILY MEMBER FOR TWENTY YEARS, SUDDENLY BEGAN TO DISTANCE HIMSELF FROM US.

SOME NIGHTS HE DIDN'T EVEN COME HOME AT ALL.

OR, IF HE DID, HE WAS COMPLETELY DRUNK.

WHAT? I'M AS SOBER AS A GODDAMN PRIEST.

BUT OUR MOTHER, SHE DIDN'T WANT US KIDS TO KNOW THERE WERE PROBLEMS AND TRIED TO HIDE HER SUFFERING FROM US. TO US, SHE WAS ALWAYS THE SAME MOTHERLY PERSON, LAUGHING, TENDER, YOUNG.

DADDY'S FINE, HE'S JUST...TIRED.

HE'S BEEN WORKING REALLY LONG HOURS AT THE RESTAURANT LATELY. THAT'S ALL.

OUR MOM DIDN'T EVEN MIND WHEN MY OLDER BROTHERS AND SISTERS JOINED THE SOCIALIST YOUTH GROUP*; SHE EVEN LET THEM HAVE THEIR BIG MEETINGS AT OUR HOUSE.

Brider un shvester fun arbet un noyt, tsezeyt un tseshpreyt iz greyt, zi flatert fun shvue, a shvue, af lebn...

Ale vos zaynen tsuzamen, tsuzamen, di fon Tsuzamen, fun tsorn, fun blut iz zi royt, un toyt!**

SING IT!

BUT MANY TIMES, WE'D HEAR THE HORSE-DRAWN CART PULL UP UNDER THE WINDOW, A SURE SIGN DAD WAS COMING HOME DRUNK AGAIN.

THERE'S NO COMMIE SONGS ALLOWED.

GET THE HELL OUT OF MY HOUSE!

IN MY PATRIOTICALLY POLISH ABODE.

OUT!

* Called "Tsukunft," it means "future" in Yiddish, the youth wing of the socialist party, led by the youths themselves and some 15,000 strong.
** Brothers and sisters, in toil and struggle / All who are scattered far and wide / Come together, the flag is ready

Until one day, what had to happen HAPPENED

IT WAS THE TIME OF THE SHORT SUMMER NIGHTS.

MOM, IS EVERYTHING OKAY? YOU'RE NOT AT WORK?

EVERYTHING'S MORE THAN OKAY. PERFECT.

YOUR UNCLE ITZ FROM NEW JERSEY JUST SENT ME ONE HUNDRED AMERICAN DOLLARS INHERITANCE.

BUT WHAT ABOUT DAD WHAT IF HE GETS TO THE MONEY IF HE HEARS ABOUT IT HE'LL JUST TAKE IT AND DRINK IT ALL UP AND HE MIGHT NOT EVER COME BACK AGAIN AND THEN WHAT'LL WE DO HE'S ALREADY SOMETIMES NOT EVEN BRINGING HIS PAYCHECKS FROM THE RESTAURANT HOME AND...

OH, DON'T WORRY. I HID IT.

I HID IT VERY, VERY WELL.

THAT NIGHT WAS ONE OF THOSE WHEN FATHER DIDN'T SHOW UP.

IT'S PAST MIDNIGHT.

HE'S NOT COMING HOME.

WHAT DO YOU WANT TO DO?

LET'S LOCK UP.

DOESN'T HE HAVE A KEY?

G'NIGHT, EVERYONE.

NOT FOR THIS LOCK.

THE NEXT MORNING WE WERE SURPRISED TO BE AWAKENED BY THE PRESENCE OF OUR NEIGHBOR MENDL THE PORTER.

SORRY, GOLDIE, I DIDN'T MEAN TO SCARE YOU BUT I WAS WALKING BY ON MY WAY TO MINYAN* AND I NOTICED THAT YOUR FRONT DOOR WAS WIDE OPEN.

I WANTED TO CHECK THAT EVERYTHING'S OKAY BY YOU.

JUST THEN THE PHONE STARTED RINGING.

NEXT THING, OUR MOTHER THREW A COAT OVER HER NIGHTGOWN, GRABBED MY TWO OLDEST SISTERS, AND RACED TO DAD'S RESTAURANT.

* An early morning gathering requiring at least ten Jewish men (and these days, sometimes men AND women) to make a quorum. Nine just won't cut it.

WHEN THEY GOT THERE THEY WERE GREETED WITH THE SIGHT OF OUR FATHER PASSED OUT ON THE FLOOR, AND LAYING NEAR HIM, A RUSSIAN WAITRESS FROM THE RESTAURANT IN AN INDECENT POSITION.

IT TURNED OUT THAT PAPA HAD FOUND THE HUNDRED DOLLARS WHEN HE BROKE IN. THEN HE LEFT US AND MADE SURE OUR MOTHER HAD NO ACCESS TO HIS PENSION. MOTHER WAS FORCED TO SELL VEGETABLES IN THE MARKET, BUT THE IDEA OF SUPPORTING SIX PEOPLE ON THAT WAS RIDICULOUS.

SO ONE MORNING MOTHER ADDRESSED ALL OF US KIDS.

I WANT THE YOUNGEST OF YOU TO GO TO WHERE YOUR FATHER LIVES WITH THE CHRISTIAN WOMAN AND WHEN YOU GET THERE, THIS IS WHAT I WANT YOU TO DO...

I WENT WITH MY SISTER.

PAPA, WE HAVE COME HERE TO ASK YOU FOR FOOD.

WITH THIS, PAPA'S NEW WOMAN ROUSED THE DOG AND CAME AFTER US WITH A POT OF BOILING WATER.

THE NEXT DAY, MOTHER SENT THE TWO OLDEST
CHILDREN, WITH THE SAME RESULT.

PAPA WENT TO THE POLICE.

THE COMMIES ARE AFTER US.

AFTER THREE YEARS IN COURT, HE WAS
SENTENCED TO A HALF YEAR IN PRISON
FOR STEALING MOTHER'S MONEY, BUT
HIS WOMAN BAILED HIM OUT AND THEY
MOVED ALL THE WAY TO GRODNO.* NOW
ALL HE WANTED WAS A "GET."** BUT OUR
MOM WOULDN'T GIVE HIM ONE.

* Grodno, a city in Western Russia/Eastern Poland. Before WWII, half of the 50,000 people who lived there were Jewish. None survived.
** Get: a written document which under Jewish religious law allows for a divorce if a) the husband presents it to the wife and b) GETS
THE WIFE'S APPROVAL!

85

WE HEARD FROM SOMEONE PASSING THROUGH TOWN FROM GRODNO THAT PAPA HAD RECENTLY CONVERTED TO THE RUSSIAN ORTHODOX FAITH.

I STARTED SINGING YIDDISH SONGS, ESPECIALLY THE SAD ONES.*

Oh, little bird

When you come to my window, sing no more

Oh, little bird

My heart is so heavy

For you can love whomever you desire

I love too, but my love finds obstacles in the way

Oh, little bird

*"Feygele" (Little Bird)

NOW, JUST THIS YEAR, OUR FAMILY WAS AGAIN ENGULFED IN TURMOIL.

FIRST, MY OLDEST SISTER PICKED UP AND MOVED TO PARIS WITH HER BOYFRIEND.

BON JER.

THE NEXT YOUNGEST SISTER STARTED WORKING FOR THE NON-JEWISH CHAIRMAN OF THE TRADE UNION.

THE SISTER JUST OLDER THAN ME STARTED STUDYING BOOKKEEPING AT NIGHT SCHOOL.

THEN, THE SISTER AT THE UNION STARTED GOING OUT WITH THE BOSS.

AND ONE DAY, SHE COMES HOME, PACKS HER BAGS, AND DISAPPEARS, GIVING HER JOB AT THE UNION TO MY SISTER THE BOOKKEEPER.

YOU'LL LIKE IT, IT'S EASY.

* Flowery Polish language

NOT LONG AFTER SHE STARTED THERE, THE CHAIRMAN CALLED HER ASIDE.

I BET YOU'D LIKE TO SEE WHAT'S BECOME OF YOUR BIG SISTER.

PIOTR AND I ARE MOVING TO WARSAW, AND WE'RE NEVER COMING HOME AGAIN.

WITH THAT, MY SISTER THE BOOKKEEPER QUIT ON THE SPOT, AND MOVED TO PARIS AS WELL.

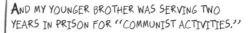

BON JER!

MEANWHILE, MY OLDEST BROTHER WAS SERVING TWO YEARS IN THE POLISH ARMY.

AND MY YOUNGER BROTHER WAS SERVING TWO YEARS IN PRISON FOR "COMMUNIST ACTIVITIES."

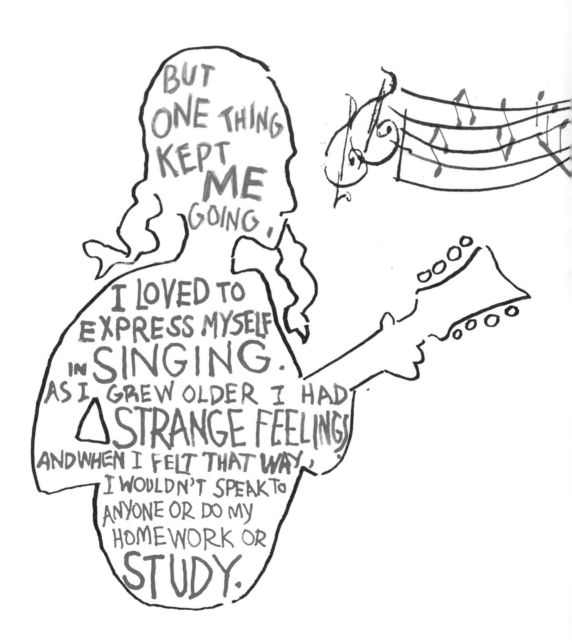

I STARTED MAKING UP MY OWN SONGS, AND THEY JUST
KEPT GETTING BETTER AND BETTER. I WAS AMAZED.

I WOULD come home from School and Sing for HOURS without Stopping.

WHICH LEAVES ME AS THE ONLY ONE AT HOME WITH MY MOTHER.

WE BOTH WORK. I'M A CLERK AND MY MOM HAS BEEN FORCED TO DO HOUSEWORK FOR A FRIEND.

HERE!

I EARN A GRAND TOTAL OF THREE ZŁOTYS A WEEK

HERE!

OF COURSE, I GIVE ALL MY MONEY TO MY MOTHER.

EVEN THOUGH AT MY AGE...

I'D LIKE SOME MONEY FOR MYSELF.

I NOTICED MOTHER SIMPLY BEGAN TO FADE AWAY DAY BY DAY.

95

SOME TEA?

THANKS, MOM.

YOU KNOW, OUR FAMILY IS SPLIT RIGHT DOWN THE MIDDLE, WE ARE IN A STALEMATE.

THERE ARE SIX OF YOU CHILDREN,

AND YOU'RE EVENLY DIVIDED.

HERE SHE GOES AGAIN!

"ENTRIES WILL BE COMPLETELY AND TOTALLY ANONYMOUS"

LET'S SEE, MY OLDEST SISTER IS STILL IN PARIS AND SENDS MONEY TO MOM—SO SHE'S ON MOM'S SIDE.

MOM ✓   DAD

THE SECOND OLDEST, WHO RAN AWAY WITH THE CHAIRMAN AND WHO WE HAVEN'T HEARD A WORD FROM—SHE'S WITH DAD.

MOM   DAD ✓

THE OLDER BROTHER, THE SOLDIER, NOW HE'S A TAILOR—HE SUPPORTS MOM TOO.

MOM ✓   DAD

BUT MY YOUNGER BROTHER—A TOTAL LAZYBONES— ONE MORE VOTE FOR DAD.

MOM   DAD ✓

THE SISTER JUST OLDER THAN ME, THE BOOKKEEPER, SHE'S IN PARIS TOO, WORKING WITH THE ZIONIST COMMUNISTS, AND MOM AND HER ARE STILL TIGHT

MOM ✓   DAD

WHICH LEAVES ME, TO WEIGH IN ON THIS SIDE OR THAT SIDE.

AND, IN FACT, I FEEL I MYSELF AM TIED, I MYSELF AM HANGING IN THE BALANCE.

DON'T GET ME WRONG—I AM VERY GRATEFUL TO MY HARD-WORKING MOTHER AND APPRECIATE ALL HER VERY GREAT SELF-SACRIFICE AND LOVE FOR ME.

BUT STILL, IN MY DREAMS, IN MY THOUGHTS, IN MY WHOLE LIFE, I AM OVERCOME WITH LONGING...

... for my father

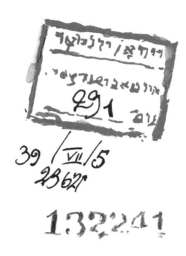

THE RULE BREAKER*
11-and-a-half-year-old girl

* Unlike the others, this entrant broke the rules THREE times when she submitted her autobiography:
1) by entering too young; 2) by including a photo; and 3) by revealing her name, Beba Epstein.

בעבע עסטיין

= אױטאביאגרא =
פיע

זיבער קל   עול· יאר 1933-ה
יי דיצע עול אויף בבקאװע 5 א

זעטע: דיעעער
25

WHAT THEY DON'T KNOW WON'T HURT THEM.

ONE THING'S FOR SURE, I WAS A VERY NAUGHTY CHILD. I WOULD BREAK EVERYTHING IN SIGHT. WHEN I WAS TWO I CRAWLED UP ON THE BUFFET AND PULLED OPEN THE DISPLAY CASE AND ALL THE PLATES FELL OUT AND BROKE.

I WAS SURE I'D BE YELLED AT, BUT INSTEAD EVERYONE STARTED TO LAUGH SO HARD THAT I BEGAN TO LAUGH TOO.

BUT AFTER, MY ZEYDE* SAID,

BEBA, I HAVE SOMETHING VERY IMPORTANT TO TELL YOU.

MY ZEYDE WAS SO SERIOUS AND SO RELIGIOUS HE ACTUALLY SLEPT IN A HAT.

YOU MUST ALWAYS BE VERY RELIGIOUS.

IF NOT, GOD WILL SPANK YOU WITH IRON RODS.

* Grandpa

110

FROM THEN ON, WHENEVER I DID ANYTHING WRONG, I'D HIDE SO GOD WOULD NOT SEE ME.

 "DO NOT THINK THAT ONLY EXTRAORDINARY PEOPLE CAN WIN, TALK ABOUT WHAT'S IMPORTANT TO YOU."

I'LL NEVER FORGET MY FIRST MOVIE.

IT WAS "UNCLE TOM'S CABIN."

THE WAY THE BLACK PEOPLE SUFFERED, IT WAS SO HORRIBLE.

AT SCHOOL, WE HAD TO READ THE BOOK,* AND LEARNED HOW, ON THE BOAT FROM AFRICA, IT WAS "WORSE THAN HELL." OUR TEACHER THEN TOLD US ABOUT THE TRAGEDY OF THE SCOTTSBORO BOYS** AND HOW THEY'RE MAKING A YIDDISH PLAY ABOUT IT IN WARSAW.***

* Russian-Jewish writer Isaac Dik's 1868 (very loose) Yiddish translation.
** The 1931 case of the Scottsboro Boys—nine African American teenagers falsely accused of raping two white women, one of the most egregious cases of racism and injustice in American history.
*** "Mississippi," a 1935 play by Polish-Yiddish writer Leyb Malakh, the first literary treatment of this horrible event in any language.

* When Max Weinreich visited America on a fellowship in the early 1930s, he spent most of his time traveling around the South and getting to know and connect with faculty at several of the traditionally Black colleges and universities, and, as a result, he invited several leading African American scholars to teach and learn in the Yiddishuanian capital of Vilna—an event that was all set to happen if not for the disruptive events of September 1, 1939.

117

SINCE MY FIRST MOVIE, I GO TO MOVIES ALL THE TIME,
ALL BY MYSELF. AND THE THEATER TOO.

BEBA, I HEARD FROM AUNTY RIFKA THAT
YOUR COUSIN FREYDKA'S WRITING AN
AUTOBIOGRAPHY FOR YIVO THAT COULD WIN
HER 150 ZŁOTYS!

MOM WAS SUCH A "BUTTINSKI."

BUT RIFKA SAYS IT HAS TO BE SERIOUS, NOT ABOUT RADIO OR MOVIES OR MAGAZINES...

AND MY OLDER COUSIN FREYDKA? DON'T EVEN GET ME STARTED.

TOO BAD YOU'RE NOT SIXTEEN,

YOU'RE SUCH A CLEVER GIRL.

YOU HAVE TO BE SIXTEEN TO ENTER.

EVERYONE AND EVERYTHING WAS ALWAYS TELLING ME WHAT TO DO, AS IF I NEEDED ADVICE!

AS THE PURVEYOR OF YOUR BELOVED... COD LIVER OIL

I'M TELLING YOU YOU BETTER FOLLOW THE RULES...

BECAUSE YOU KNOW WHAT HAPPENS WHEN YOU DISOBEY.

OBEY THE RULES? LIKE HELL I'LL OBEY THE RULES. I'LL WRITE THE TRUTH, THAT'S THE RULES FOR ME.

SERIOUS? HMMM...

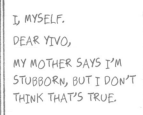

I, MYSELF.

DEAR YIVO,

MY MOTHER SAYS I'M STUBBORN, BUT I DON'T THINK THAT'S TRUE.

MOM, LOOK HOW AWESOME THIS SUMMER DRESS LOOKS ON ME.

TA-DA!

I'VE JUST GOT TO WEAR IT TO SCHOOL TODAY.

IT'S SNOWING AND FREEZING.

YOU'LL DIE OF A COLD.

AND YOU KNOW WHAT ELSE, MOM, IT'S SO GREAT LOOKING, I'M NOT EVEN GONNA WEAR A COAT.

I KNOW YOU THINK IT'S WARM OUT, BUT IF YOU INSIST ON WEARING THAT DRESS...

AT LEAST WEAR A COAT!

COAT SHMOAT!

WHAT'S THE POINT OF WEARING A BEAUTIFUL DRESS LIKE THIS IF PEOPLE ON THE STREET CAN'T SEE IT?

AND MOM!

BESIDES, I DON'T GET COLD.

AS A RESULT OF THAT LITTLE WALK, I
WAS SICK FOR FIVE WEEKS.

THE DOCTORS AT THE JEWISH HOSPITAL SAID A CASE LIKE MINE HAPPENS ONLY ONCE LIKE EVERY SEVEN YEARS.

WHEN I GOT OUT, I HAD TO SPEND
MY SUMMER AT THE HEALTH COLONY IN
NOWA WILEJKA.

I LIKED IT THERE, AND WITH ALL
THE SWIMMING AND HIKING AND
SUNBATHING, I FINALLY GOT BETTER.

BUT WHEN I CAME BACK TO SCHOOL, MY NOSE
AND THROAT WERE STILL BOTHERING ME SO
MUCH I WENT TO THE UNIVERSITY CLINIC. THEY
SAID I HAD TO GO TO THE HEALTH COLONY
AGAIN.

AND GUESS WHAT? IT WAS EVEN BETTER THAN
BEFORE. WE SUNG AND PUT ON PLAYS.

BY THE END OF THE SUMMER I CAME HOME
FEELING GREAT.

AT FIRST...

I EVEN GOT THE STARRING ROLE IN THE SCHOOL PLAY, "MOTL PEYSL DEM CHASN."*

IMAGINE IT,
ME, A GIRL
PLAYING MOTL!

* *Motl, Peysl the Cantor's Son* was Sholem Aleichem's last novel, left unfinished at the time of his death. Published in two parts in 1907 and subtitled *The Writings of an Orphan Boy*, it describes the trials of life in both Eastern Europe and the "New World," of America. It was turned into a play not long after publication and became a staple of Yiddish theater. Interestingly, Aleichem makes Motl an aspiring and talented young cartoonist. A cartoonist caught between two worlds.

BUT ON OPENING NIGHT, I HAD SUCH TERRIBLE STOMACH PAINS I HAD TO MISS THE PERFORMANCE. AND NOW IT'S MY TEETH THAT ARE GIVING ME TROUBLE. THAT'S NO FUN.

SO IT LOOKS LIKE I'M GOING TO HEALTH CAMP AGAIN THIS SUMMER.

THE THING IS, THEY LOVE ME AT HOME, BUT THEY DON'T UNDERSTAND ME.

IT SEEMS LIKE THE ONLY TIME THEY TAKE ME SERIOUSLY IS WHEN I'M SICK.

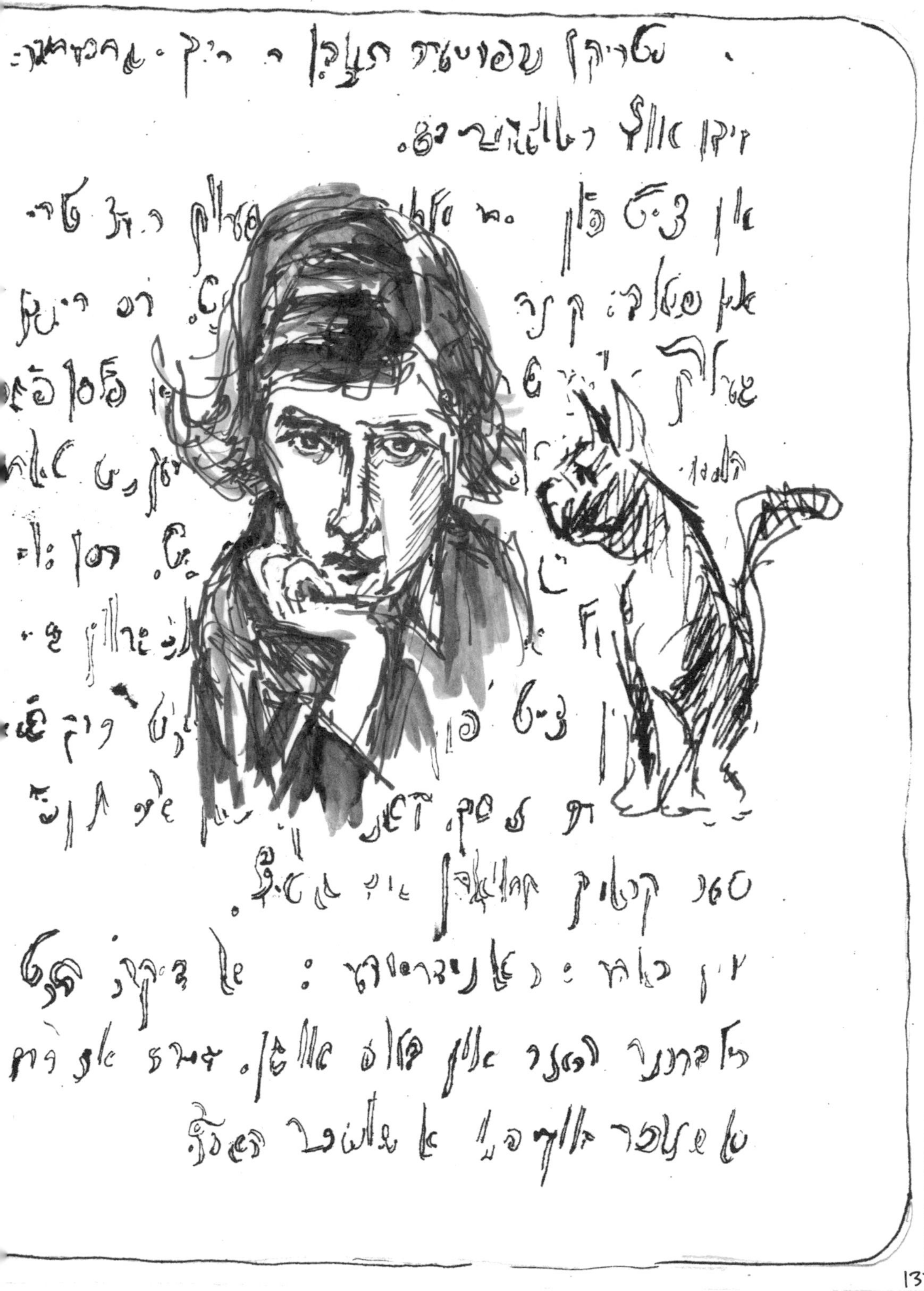

THE BOY WHO LIKED A GIRL

20-year-old boy

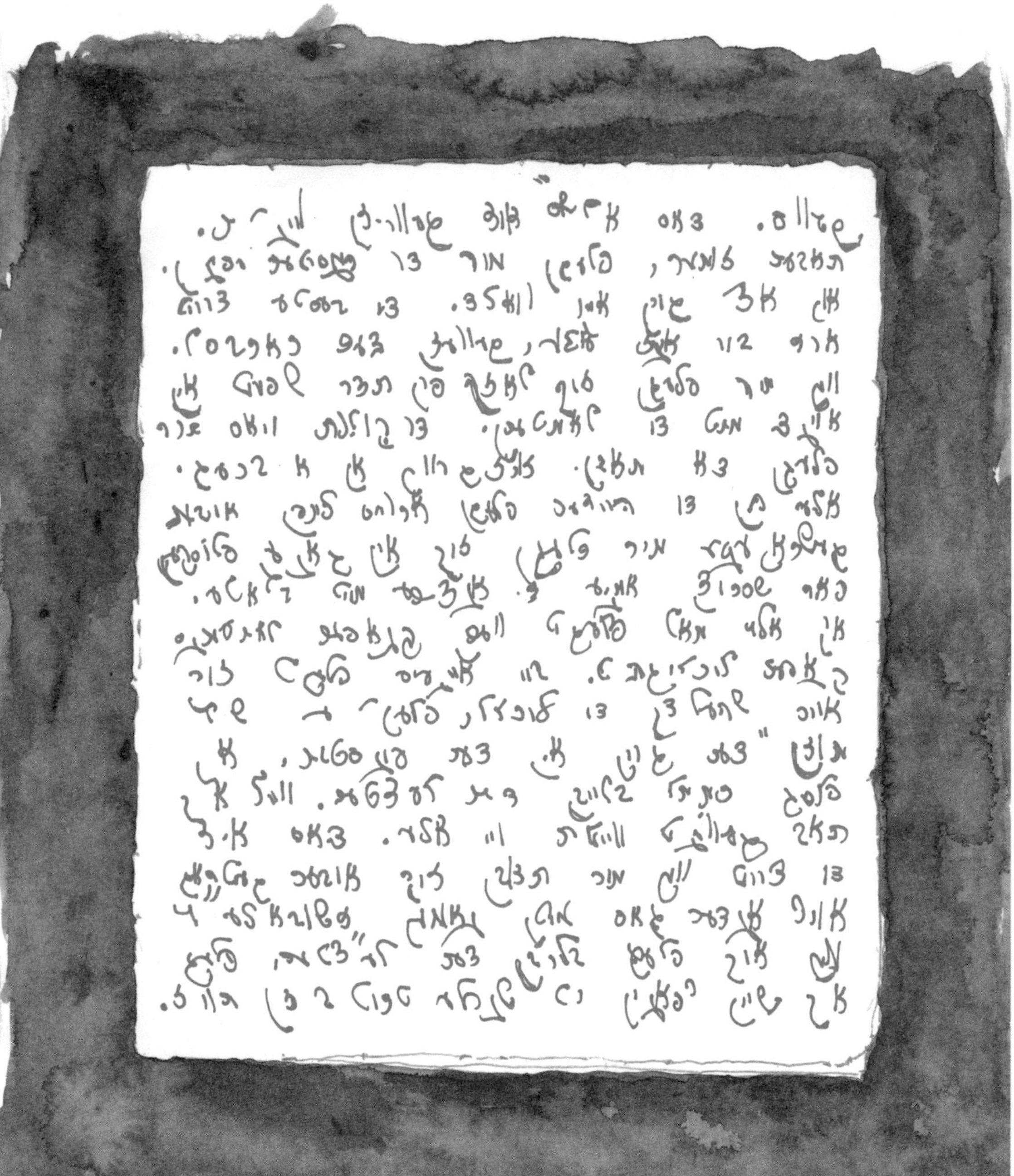

MY LIFE WITH MY FRIENDS
WAS GREAT. I WAS
ALWAYS THE BOSS. WE
LIVED FOR THE MOMENT,
NEVER THINKING OF
TOMORROW.

BUT I'M NOT GOING TO WRITE ABOUT MY LIFE WITH THEM. INSTEAD, I'M WRITING ABOUT MY LIFE WITH GIRLS—ONE IN PARTICULAR.

FOR THE PURPOSES OF THIS ANONYMOUS AUTOBIOGRAPHY, I'LL CALL HER "M."

IT ALL STARTS WHEN, FOR THE FIRST TIME EVER, I DITCHED MY FRIENDS TO BE WITH A GIRL. WITH "M.".

CATCH YOU LATER.

I'D COME HOME FROM SCHOOL, AND SHE'D BE WAITING FOR ME.

I'D RUSH THROUGH MY HOMEWORK, MAKING LOTS OF MISTAKES. AND WHEN I FINISHED, AND LOOKED UP AT HER, IN MY HEART I WOULD FEEL...STRANGE. UNTIL SHE STARTED TALKING, THAT IS.

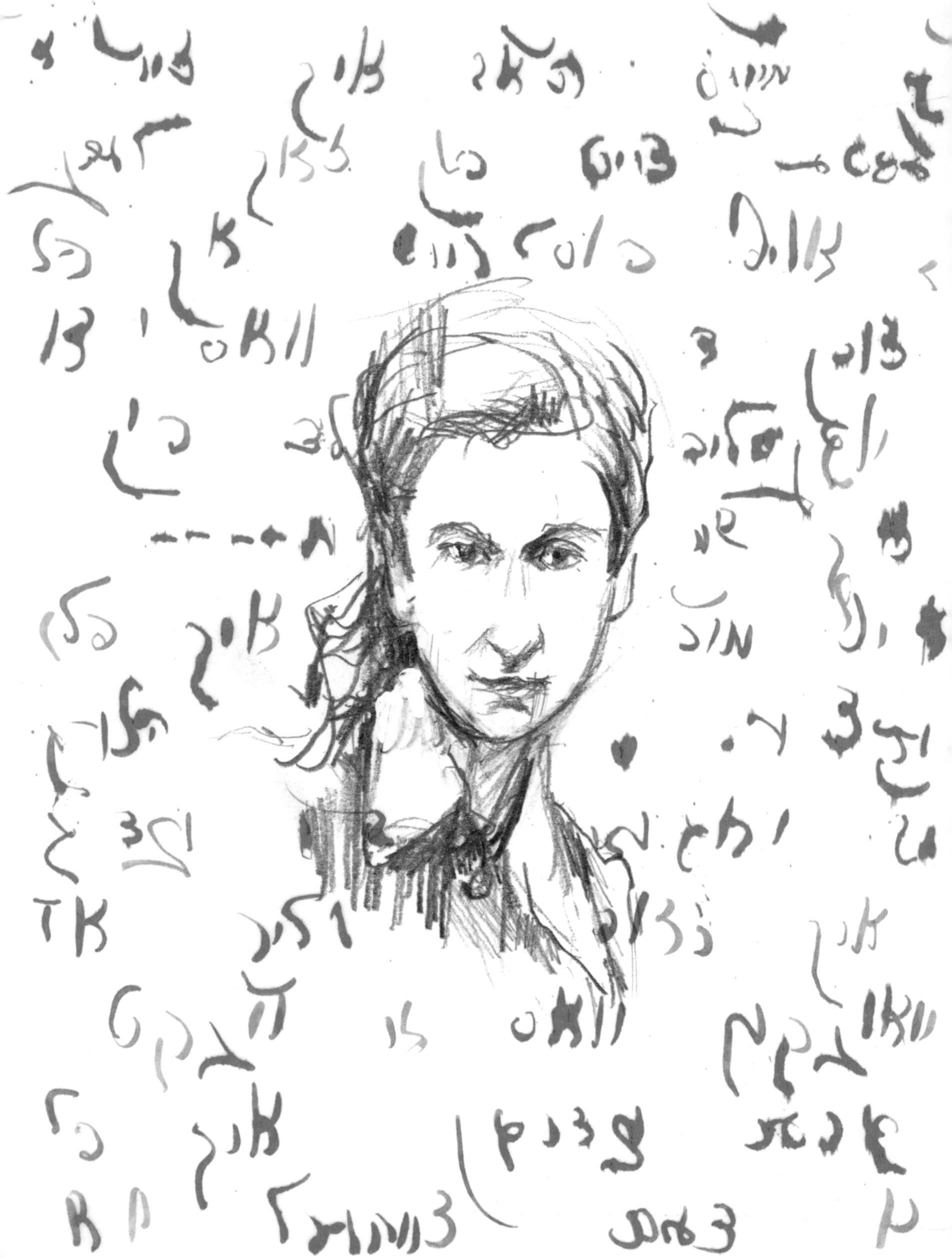

NO QUESTION, "M" AND I DEVELOPED A RELATIONSHIP THAT COULD HAVE BECOME SOMETHING TRULY IMPORTANT.

BUT SOMETHING HAPPENED THAT TORE US APART AND LED US TO FORGET ABOUT EACH OTHER FOR A LONG, LONG TIME.

ONE FINE MORNING, I HEARD SOME BAD NEWS— "M" WAS MOVING FAR AWAY TO THE OTHER SIDE OF TOWN.

WHEN WE SAID GOODBYE, MY EYES WEREN'T CRYING, BUT MY SOUL WAS.

KHATKL, YOU HAVE TO COME VISIT. I WILL NEVER FORGET YOU.

AFTER SHE LEFT, I FELL IN WITH A DIFFERENT CROWD AND STARTED ACTING UP IN SCHOOL, TORMEMTING MY TEACHERS. WE STAGED A STRIKE AND WHEN ONE BOY, YESHOA, DIDN'T WANT TO TAKE PART, THE THUGS IN OUR GROUP TIED HIM UP AND CARRIED HIM OUT THE DOOR.

I WANTED TO FOLLOW MY NEW GANG TO THE PUBLIC HIGH SCHOOL, BUT MY FATHER WOULDN'T HEAR OF IT.

NO SON OF MINE IS GOING TO ANY POLISH SCHOOL.

"M."

MY FATHER MADE ME GO TO THE RELIGIOUS SCHOOL, BUT IT DIDN'T MATTER. AS SOON AS SCHOOL WAS OVER, I'D STUFF MY YARMULKE IN MY POCKET AND THREE STREETCARS, A BUS, AND A LONG WALK LATER, I'D BE HANGING OUT OUTSIDE THE YIDDISH SOCIALIST FOLK SHUL* WHERE "M" NOW WENT.

BUT SHE WOULDN'T SPEAK TO ME. WAS IT BECAUSE I DIDN'T BECOME A COMMUNIST AND START EATING PORK? WAS IT BECAUSE I COULDN'T GO TO THE DINNER DANCE HER SOCIALIST YOUTH GROUP HAD ON YOM KIPPUR?**

I WANTED TO REMIND HER OF OUR LOVE, OUR PAST. I KNEW IF SHE'D JUST SPEAK TO ME FOR A MINUTE, SHE'D FORGET ALL THAT POLITICS STUFF AND THINGS WOULD BE LIKE THEY USED TO BE. BUT NO.

I BIT MY LIPS AND TRIED TO FORGET HER.

"M."

"M?"

"M!"

* Progressive, liberal, secular education—but informed by the spirit and feeling of the culture of Yiddishuania, a kind of engaged Jewish identity outside of simply religiosity.
** Yes, this extremely sacrilegious practice (on the most holy day of the year, and a fasting day no less!) was practiced by many extremely radical co-religionists in Yiddishuania as a form of rebellion. See page 115 of *From That Place and Time* by Lucy Dawidowicz if you don't believe me!

WHEN I STARTED AT THE JEWISH HIGH SCHOOL, MY OLD FRIENDS INVITED ME BACK INTO THE FOLD, BUT I QUICKLY REALIZED IT WASN'T SO MUCH THAT THEY MISSED ME, IT WAS MORE THAT AS SOON AS THEY FIGURED THAT "M" AND ME WERE THROUGH, THEY WANTED TO USE ME TO GET TO "M" THEMSELVES. YOU SEE, WE ALL LOVED "M." WHAT REALLY BUGGED ME, THOUGH, WAS HOW MUCH BORUKH AND GABRIEL KEPT TRYING TO GET ME TO GO AFTER OTHER GIRLS, TO GET ME OUT OF THE WAY.

151

ONE MORNING, I WOKE UP SUPER EARLY AND DECIDED I HAD TO GO FOR A WALK IN THE WOODS.

NEVER WAS I SO DRAWN TO THE WOODS AS ON THIS DAY.

I WENT RIGHT OUT. I DIDN'T SEE ANYONE. NOT EVEN "M." NOBODY. I DIDN'T WANT TO.

153

INSTEAD, I MET A YESHIVA BOKHER* WITH A PALE FACE, SITTING ABSORBED IN A HOLY BOOK.

* Student of an extremely religious school, usually a boarding school; could be anyone from a peach fuzz–bearded nine-year-old to a full-bearded seventy-three-year-old, distinguished by their obsessive commitment to intellectual "cage-wrestling," sincere piety, profound self-questioning, and a tendency to squint.

* The school where yeshiva bokhers hang out, focused on religious texts, the Torah, the Talmud, and the Gemore, approximately a zillion pages of commentary on the aforementioned. Yeshivot (the plural) come in many flavors, from quiet and intense in fancy suits to yelling and pounding tables in fraying black gabardine, and in the early years of the twentieth century they are bursting at the seams with new angles and dimensions, from the mystical to the scientific to the intellectual, a renegade spark of creativity that flourished and then vanished.

THIS EXPRESSION, "TO LIVE INDEPENDENTLY," IT RESOUNDED IN MY EARS. THIS WAS A BIG DEAL.
NO MORE INTERFERENCE FROM HOME, FROM MY FATHER! AT THAT MOMENT, I COULD SEE MY
WHOLE FUTURE. I WOULD BE AN INDEPENDENT PERSON! I WOULD LIVE BY MYSELF, ALONE, IN THE
BIG WORLD. I SAID IT OVER AND OVER TO MYSELF.

157

I DANCED WITH JOY.

THAT VERY MOMENT, I DECIDED TO GO.

AT SCHOOL, I DIDN'T EVEN TELL MY FRIENDS THAT THIS WAS GOING TO BE MY LAST DAY IN TRESTINA.*

AND THAT EVENING, WHEN I TOLD MY PARENTS, THEY WERE HAPPY, ESPECIALLY WHEN THEY HEARD IT WAS TO BE COMPLETELY PAID FOR BY THE ROV.**

THE NIGHT I WENT, THE MOON WAS FULL.

* Yiddishuanian village of Trzcianne. In 1897 it was inhabited by 2,266 Jews, who made up 98 percent of the population—the most Jewish town in the region. Only 25 survived WWII, and they all immigrated to the United States as soon as they could.
** The chief rabbi of the yeshiva in question.

WHEN I ARRIVED IN BIALYSTOCK* MY HEAD WAS HURTING FROM SO MUCH ALL AROUND ME.

AT THE YESHIVA THE BOYS DAVENED SO LOUDLY I WAS SCARED. I HAD NO IDEA WHAT I WAS SUPPOSED TO DO.

* The largest city in northeastern Poland, 50 percent Jewish at the time.

I FROZE AT THE DOOR FOR A FULL TEN MINUTES, UNTIL FINALLY THE BOKHER FROM THE WOODS APPROACHED ME.

THE BOKHER GAVE ME TEFILLIN* TO DAVEN WITH. IN THE PAST WHEN I WAS FORCED TO PRAY MY MIND WANDERED. BUT NOW EVERYTHING ELSE VANISHED.

NO QUESTION ABOUT IT, I WAS A BORN BOKHER!

* Jewish ritual prayer accoutrements: two small leather boxes with scripture inside, one wrapped around the arm, the other situated on the forehead.

AFTERWARD, I FOLLOWED THE BOKHER DOWN THE STREET TO THE KITCHEN FOR SOME LUNCH. ON THE WAY, WE PASSED SOME GIRLS WALKING ON THE SIDEWALK.

JUST TO BE FRIENDLY, I SLOWED DOWN AND STARTED TALKING TO THEM.

DO NOT EVER LET ANY WOMAN WALK WITH YOU.

THE BOKHER GRABBED MY SLEEVE AND STARTED YELLING AND THE GIRLS STARTED LAUGHING. I WAS EMBARRASSED. I DIDN'T LIKE WHAT HE WAS DOING, BUT I SWALLOWED MY ANGER.

IT WAS HARD FOR ME TO ADAPT TO SUCH A LIFE. BACK HOME, I LIKED TO SPEND A FEW NIGHTS A WEEK OUT IN THE WOODS, MAYBE WITH A GIRL, BREATHING IN THE FRESH AIR—WHICH AS YOU KNOW IS VERY GOOD FOR A PERSON.

BUT THERE, I WAS IN A SMALL DARK ROOM WHERE I STUDIED DAY AND NIGHT. TRUE, I TOOK TO IT WITH ENTHUSIASM. I'D SIT WITH MY HEAD BURIED IN THE GEMORE* FOR HOURS ON END.

SO MUCH THAT IF MY GANG, EVEN THE RUFFIANS AND SCAMPS, SAW ME, THEY'D HAVE SWORN I'D BEEN A BOKHER FOREVER.

HE'S SO ** FRUM!

UNREAL!

HIS HEAD'S ALWAYS IN A HOLY BOOK

I ALWAYS THOUGHT HE WAS WEIRD

* Commentary on commentary on commentary on the Bible.
** Super-ultra-extremely religious to the max.

BUT NO.

TRUE, I'D BE SITTING WITH MY HEAD IN MY HANDS, THINKING.

BUT NOT ABOUT TALMUD OR GEMORE.

I WAS THINKING ABOUT WAY MORE IMPORTANT THINGS.

WHEN SUMMER ROLLED AROUND, AND THE WEATHER GOT WARM, I'D FIND MYSELF MAKING UP EXCUSES TO LEAVE THE YESHIVA.

I'VE GOT TO GO VISIT MY SICK AUNT ACROSS TOWN.

REALLY???

I THOUGHT IT WAS YOUR UNCLE THAT WAS SO SICK.

I DIDN'T KNOW YOU HAD AN AUNT IN TOWN?

Agfa

IN THE STREET I WOULD SEE PEOPLE STROLLING, GIRLS AND BOYS, SOME WALKING IN THE PARK, OTHERS LYING DOWN WITH THEIR D IN THE OTHER'S LAP. AT SUCH ME I WOULD BE SEIZED WITH LONG   I WOULD REMEMBER LEANING MY HEAD ON "M." HOW WARM HER BREASTS WERE WHEN SHE LEANED ON ME.

BEHIND ME A RADIO WAS PLAYING, BEAUTIFUL ROMANTIC WORDS.

How Deep is the Ocean? How High is the Sky?

My fantasy of what the yeshiva would be like was different. I thought I would be living a pure scholarly life. Living alone in a nice apartment, eating at my own expense, what I wanted, going to the theater, enjoying the world. But it all came to nothing. I was as submissive as a slave. In the winter it was worse, at night on Shabbes, I would wait in the cold, quickly grab dinner in the afternoon and then go back to study some more. Long gone were the days when on winter Shabbes nights I would go visit "M." No. Today, everything is gone. My youth is gone.

WHEN PURIM* ARRIVED, WE ALL HAD TO GO TO THE MASHGIAKH'S** HOUSE.

NOW, WE SING!

SURE, I SANG, BUT WITHOUT A DROP OF FEELING.

* Late winter Jewish holiday commemorating dodging getting annihilated (for a change) by getting dressed up in costumes and getting sarcastic.
** The boss of all that is right and pious in a yeshivah, and with the authority to enforce it.

I WOULD RATHER HAVE BEEN SINGING A TANGO*
OR A HIT TUNE. THAT WOULD HAVE RELIEVED
THE HEAVINESS IN MY HEART. HELPED ME
FORGET MY SUFFERING JUST A LITTLE.
INSTEAD MY WHOLE GOING TO YESHIVA
HAD TURNED INTO SLEEPING ON
A TABLE, WASHING ONCE
A WEEK ON FRIDAY WITH
WATER FROM A BARREL,
AND LOST YOUTH.

* Dance music popularized in the vice-ridden alleys of Buenos Aires (often vice-ridden thanks to the expatriate Yiddishuanian vice-mongers, thank you very much!).

I MADE UP MY MIND. THE NEXT MORNING, I GOT UP EARLY.

I WAS SO FULL OF JOY AND PAIN I COULDN'T SLEEP.

IT WAS POURING WITH RAIN, BUT THIS DIDN'T STOP ME. I CREPT OUT OF THE YESHIVA LIKE A THIEF.

I WENT FAST. IT WAS HARD FOR ME TO CARRY SUCH HEAVY VALISES SO FAR, BUT THERE WAS NO WAY AROUND IT.

I WAS LONGING FOR MY LOST YOUTH, AND THIS KEPT ME GOING.

THERE WAS NO BUS. I RAN UNDER THE SHELTER SO I WOULDN'T GET SOAKED.

I WAS SO COLD I STILL SHIVER EVEN TODAY.

I WAS TIRED, SICK, ANGRY, AND DESPERATE. FINALLY AT 7:30 THE BUS PULLED UP.

BUT MY WAY WAS BLOCKED BY TWO YESHIVA BOKHERIM WHO HAD BEEN SENT BY THE MASHGIAKH TO BRING ME BACK.

THEY PROMISED OVER AND OVER THAT THERE WOULD BE NO MORE SUFFERING FOR ME.

YOU'LL GET ALL THE FOOD YOU WANT.

AND SEE THE BEST DOCTORS IN TOWN.

AND HOT.

YES, ALL THAT DELICIOUS FOOD YOU GET WILL BE HOT.

OH, AND YOU WON'T HAVE TO SLEEP ON A TABLE ANYMORE.

ALL I COULD DO WAS STAMP MY FOOT.

NO.

NOW TWO MORE OF THEM CAME TO STOP ME FROM LEAVING.

I DIDN'T WANT TO GO BACK. I WOULD GO HOME.

I WOULD GO FIND MY YOUTH.

BUT I COULDN'T SAY THIS TO THEM, THEY WOULD HAVE STONED ME.

NO!

I DON'T REMEMBER HOW, BUT SOMEHOW I GOT PAST THEM AND ONTO THE BUS.

I SAT AS IF ON PINS AND NEEDLES. I WANTED THE BUS TO GET MOVING SO THE MASHGIAKH HIMSELF SHOULD NOT COME.

WHEN THE BUS FINALLY STARTED UP I BREATHED A SIGH OF RELIEF.

BUT DELIBERATELY, AS IF OUT OF SPITE, SOMEONE NEEDED SOMETHING.

AND THE BUS SCREECHED TO A STOP.

I WAS TERRIFIED.

THE FOUR BOKHERS YELLED AT ME THROUGH THE WINDOWS TO COME BACK, THAT EVERYTHING WOULD BE BETTER.

AND BELIEVE IT OR NOT, AS I SAT LOOKING AT THEM IN THE RAIN, I ACTUALLY FELT SORRY THAT I WAS LEAVING AND THAT THEY STILL HAD TO STAY.

I FINALLY CALMED DOWN WHEN THE BUS WAS OUT OF BIELSK. MY SOUL FLEW AS THE FIELDS FLEW BY.

THE WHOLE RIDE HOME, I WAS THINKING OF MY LOST YOUTH. ALL I WANTED WAS TO REGAIN MY YOUTH. I WAS GOING TO GET IT BACK.

WHEN I GOT OFF THE BUS, A CROWD FELL ON ME WITH QUESTIONS. "WHAT, NO LONGER A BOKHER? WHAT'S WITH YOU?" AND THEN I SAW HER, "M." BUT SHE SHOT ME A COLD LOOK. I LOOKED AT HER ASKANCE, AS A YESHIVA BOKHER DOES. WHAT WAS I SUPPOSED TO DO, GO OVER AND SHAKE HER HAND? I WOULD HAVE BEEN EXCOMMUNICATED, AN UNBELIEVER. BUT AS SHE TURNED AWAY, I UNDERSTOOD THAT SHE WAS THE REAL REASON I'D COME HOME.

MY FATHER TOOK ONE LOOK AT ME AND ASKED, "ARE YOU ILL?" I COLLAPSED ON THE SOFA AND TOLD HIM EVERYTHING. HE ACCEPTED MY STORY, AS LONG AS I PROMISED TO KEEP UP MY RELIGIOUS STUDIES AT HOME.

THAT NIGHT I SAW MY OLD FRIEND GABRIEL.

WHAT'S BEEN GOING ON?

NOT MUCH, SAME OLD SAME OLD.

EXCEPT, OH, I ALMOST FORGOT TO TELL YOU, "M'S" GOING OUT WITH BORUKH.

FOR WHOM IS "M" FORSAKING ME? WHY? IS BORUKH SMARTER OR MORE HANDSOME THAN I AM?

MY HEART WAS FULL OF TEARS. I WENT TO THE WOODS.

I POURED OUT EVERYTHING TO THE TREES.
I TOLD EVERYTHING. EVERYTHING! I WAS SEIZED
WITH A DESIRE TO SING MY SORROWS.
THE TREES TREMBLED IN THE BREEZE AS IF THEY WERE
AFRAID I WOULD UNLEASH MY ANGER ON THEM.

NOW, AT LAST, MY DAVENING FELT RIGHT. I WAS
HAPPY ONLY THE TREES COULD HEAR ME.

FINALLY I LEARNED THAT THERE HAD BEEN ESTABLISHED IN VILNA A JEWISH INSTITUTE SOLICITING AUTOBIOGRAPHIES.

AND BECAUSE I BELIEVE THAT SOMETHING SHOULD COME OUT OF SO MUCH SUFFERING, I'VE WRITTEN THIS. AFTER ALL, ONE GOES THROUGH TUNNELS THAT ARE 100 KM LONG AND THEY DO END. AND THEN, ONE EMERGES INTO THE LIGHT AT LAST.

I DECIDED TO WRITE DOWN EVERYTHING, TO TELL EVERYTHING. BECAUSE WITH MY FRIENDS I CAN'T TALK ABOUT IT AT ALL.

Great is my suffering
Poor are my thoughts
No hand and no thought
Can you find here
But I want to ask
    something of You
Don't put this aside

Publish it for me.

THE SKATER
19-year-old girl

FOR THE PAST YEAR I'VE BEEN LOOKING AFTER A RICH WOMAN'S KIDS IN THE BIG CITY.

LET ME BEGIN BY SAYING I AM PRONE TO EXAGGERATION. THREE WEEKS AGO, I THOUGHT THAT IF ONLY MY SISTER WOULD SEND ME A PAIR OF ICE SKATES, I WOULD KNOW THAT I WAS A TRULY LUCKY PERSON. AND SHE DID!

BIG PACKAGE FROM WARSAW.

SUCH WARM CURRENTS ARE FLOWING THROUGH ME, THE FLAME, THE FIRE, COMPELS ME TO EXPRESS MYSELF FULLY. TO WRITE.

ALL WEEK, I LOOK FORWARD TO FRIDAY EVENING— WHEN I'M FINALLY FREE TO RUN TO THE RINK.

AS I SKATE, THE THOUGHTS FLOOD IN.

I SEE MY ADORABLE BABY BROTHER LYING IN BED, SICK—A SAD SMILE.

I AM NINE. DOCTORS CROWD OUR HOUSE.

HE WOULD HAVE GROWN TO BE SUCH A SPLENDID BOY, DRESSED IN A SHARP SPORT COAT WITH A CRISP WIDE COLLAR.

I WOULD SO LOVE TO HAVE HIM WITH ME NOW.

I'VE NEVER REALLY BELIEVED IN GOD, BUT AT THAT MOMENT I PRAYED, "IF YOU LET HIM LIVE, I WILL BELIEVE IN YOU."

MORE VISIONS RUSH IN.

NOW I'M THIRTEEN. THE ZIONISTS HAD RENTED KATZ'S HALL. A WHITE SHEET IS HUNG ON THE WALL AND A FILM IS PLAYING, YOUNG PEOPLE WORKING TOGETHER TO BUILD PALESTINE.

CLICK CLATTER

PALESTINE. THIS WAS FOR ME A FAIRY TALE, A DREAM OF SOMETHING BEAUTIFUL, FAR AWAY, AND MAYBE THEREFORE MAGICAL. I JOIN HASHOMER,* THE ZIONIST YOUTH GROUP—ALL THE KIDS FROM THE UPPER TIERS OF SOCIETY BELONGED.

WE ARE GATHERED AROUND KHAYE, THE LEADER. SHE'S DRESSED IN A WELL-CUT GRAY SAILOR BLOUSE, A KIND OF UNIFORM. SHE SPEAKS QUIETLY ABOUT LIFE ON A KIBBUTZ.** THEN WE ALL SING AND DANCE THE HORA.

* Hashomer Hatsa'ir, means "The Young Guard" in Hebrew. A Hebrew-centric, emigration-focused version of scouting based on British and German youth movements.
** A collective living–working settlement, could be agricultural or industrial.

190

I WAS OVERTAKEN WITH GIRLISH DREAMS. I PICTURE
MYSELF ON THE KIBBUTZ AND A HASHOMER BOY
APPROACHES ME IN THE COOL DESERT EVENING. I SEE
HIM—SHORT PANTS, A WHITE SHIRT, TANNED SKIN,
BEAUTIFUL TOUSLED HAIR.

WE LOOK AT EACH OTHER. WE ARE HAPPY. MY
HEART IS FULL OF SONG.

I IMAGINE THAT HE LOVES ME. HARD WORK ON THE KIBBUTZ, STRIVING TOGETHER TOWARD
ONE GOAL, UNITED, JOYFUL.

NOW I DREAM I'M ON MY WAY TO HAIFA.* I'M ON THE DECK OF A SHIP. IT'S EVENING. SHIMMERING GOLDEN DRESSES. I HEAR MUSIC, AN ORCHESTRA. IT'S AN EVENING OF DANCING.

THE DREAM SHINES BRIGHTLY.

* Main port city in then Palestine, now Israel.

OTHER WINDS BEGAN TO BLOW IN PROSCHNIZ.* DESPITE EVERYTHING I LOVED ABOUT HASHOMIR, I ENDED UP QUITTING. FIRST OF ALL, I COULDN'T UNDERSTAND A WORD OF HEBREW. AND ALSO, I STARTED SNEAKING AWAY TO THE WEEKLY YIDDISH LECTURES IN THE BIG ROOM AT THE PROVDISHER SYNAGOGUE, EVEN THOUGH YIDDISH WAS LOOKED DOWN UPON BY THE MORE REFINED CLASS OF PEOPLE.

BUT THE FORBIDDEN IS TEMPTING TO THE YOUNG.

THESE WERE THE MEETINGS OF THE POALEI ZION.** WE READ. WE DEBATED. WE EVEN TAUGHT EACH OTHER. EVERY EVENING ENRICHED ME AND UNCOVERED NEW TRUTHS ABOUT CULTURE AND SOCIETY, SHOWED ME THE BEST AND BEAUTIFUL.

POETS AND THINKERS AND ARTISTS FROM AS FAR AWAY AS VILNA OR WARSAW CAME AND SPOKE TO US.

AND AFTER, WE WOULD SING TOGETHER.

ONE POEM IS ENGRAVED IN MY MEMORY. "SIBERIA," THE HEROIC LIFE OF THE QUIET FIGHTER. SUCH A SPECIAL MOOD SWEPT OVER US ALL. I FELT LOVED.

* Currently known as Przasnysz, a town of about 20,000 in northeastern Poland.
** Socialist, Yiddishist, secular youth group. Rejected territorialism, Marxism, and sought to base Zionism, whether in Palestine or not, on the liberated and enlightened Jewish working class.

194

ONE OF THE LEADERS SPOKE.

THIS SHABBES, A LITTLE BEFORE SUNSET, WE ARE ALL TO MARCH THROUGH THE NEIGHBORING TOWN OF MAKOVE.*

...BUT I HAD MIXED FEELINGS.

I KNEW THAT THE MAKOVE GIRLS FROM THE HIGH-BORN TIERS OF SOCIETY WOULD LOOK DOWN ON US.

ONE GLANCE AND THEY'D SEE WE WERE FROM POALEI ZION.

I WOULD HAVE RATHER BEEN MARCHING WITH THE HASHOMIR. I WOULD HAVE FELT PROUD IN THEIR GRAY BLOUSE WITH THE BLUE NECKTIE RATHER THAN IN PZ'S WHITE SAILOR SUIT AND RED TIE. WHY? BECAUSE PEOPLE THOUGHT PZ WAS FOR THE POOR.

I FEEL ASHAMED SAYING IT, BUT EVEN THOUGH THE POALEI ZION PEOPLE TREATED ME LIKE A FRIEND, IT WAS A LIE. I WAS ROTTEN. AT SCHOOL, WHEN WE WERE OUT OF "UNIFORM," I GRAVITATED TO THE CREAM-OF-THE-CROP KIDS. I'D FEEL BETTER WHEN THEY WOULD TALK TO ME.

EVENTUALLY I GOT MY COMEUPPANCE, BUT MORE ON THAT LATER.

* Now known as Maków Mazowiecki, about fourteen miles from Proshniz, a slightly more wealthy village, interestingly the birthplace of United States Navy Admiral Hyman Rickover, the "Father of the Nuclear Navy." Despite nearly seventy years of Communist rule, Maków Mazowiecki boasts a "Hyman Rickover Street," ironic in that this was the very man who was very responsible for sealing the doom of the Soviet Union. (The street is very run-down.)

SHABBES HAD JUST STARTED WHEN
WE FINALLY MADE IT TO MAKOVE,
AND YOU SHOULD HAVE HEARD
WHAT THE JEWS WHO LIVED THERE
YELLED AT US AS WE MARCHED
THROUGH THE STREETS. I WANTED
TO DISAPPEAR.

* Pejorative for non-Jewish people, spoken by Jewish people.
** Shame on you! It's a disgrace, what must your parents think, and how did they raise you, anyway???

197

HEY,
WHERE DO YOU
THINK YOU'RE
GOING?

WHO DOES
SHE THINK
SHE IS
SKATING LIKE
SHE'S IN A
TRANCE?

IT TAKES
ALL TYPES!

IDIOT!
THERE ARE
CHILDREN
HERE!!!

ARE YOU
OKAY,
HONEY? YES,
THAT SILLY
WOMAN IS
SKATING
WITHOUT
LOOKING
WHERE SHE'S
GOING—SHE'S
VERY, VERY
NAUGHTY.

WATCH IT,
YOU ALMOST RAN
ME OVER.

IT WAS THEN THAT I REALIZED
THAT TRULY, MORE THAN ANYTHING,
I WANTED TO, I NEEDED TO, GO TO
GYMNASIUM* FOR HIGH SCHOOL.
TO BE WITH THE ELITE STUDENTS,
IN THEIR REFINED UNIFORMS, IN
ONE OF THE CLASSROOMS WITH
THE ENORMOUS WINDOWS, THE
SUN GLINTING OFF THEM IN THE
MORNING LIGHT.

* Not a place where you put on loose-fitting clothes and sweat. In middle and Eastern Europe, as well as Germany and Denmark, this is the name for an elite private school, the only gateway to the most competitive university studies and a better way of life.

AND ONE DAY, WITHOUT WARNING...

ENTER HERSHL GOLD-MAKHER!

HERSHL GOLDMAKHER ARRIVED IN TOWN AND IMMEDIATELY BECAME THE DARLING OF ALL THE GIRLS.

HE WAS FOR ME A LIVING GREETING FROM THE BEAUTIFUL LIFE—A GYMNASIUM STUDENT.

RIGHT AWAY, I STARTED TO PAY MORE ATTENTION TO MY APPEARANCE. IF I THOUGHT I LOOKED GOOD, I'D TRY TO RUN INTO HIM. IF NOT, I'D AVOID HIM.

WITH A WIDE WHITE COLLAR AND A BOOK IN HIS HAND WHEREVER HE WENT, HE WAS IRRESISTIBLE TO ME. I COULDN'T TAKE MY EYES OFF HIM.

BUT HERSHL GOLDMAKHER ONLY LOOKED AT ME FROM AFAR.*

STILL, EVEN THOUGH I KNEW THAT FOR ME, HERSHL WAS AN UNREACHABLE DREAM, I HAD TO LAY EYES ON HIM AT LEAST ONCE A DAY.

I ALSO STARTED SPYING ON ALL HIS GIRLFRIENDS, THE MOST PRESTIGIOUS GIRLS IN TOWN.

I WAS OBSESSED WITH THEIR INTELLIGENT, PALE FACES, CAREFREE, RADIANT, FULL OF HAPPINESS, THE EMBODIMENT OF ALL THAT WAS GOOD AND BEAUTIFUL. I TRIED AND TRIED TO CONVINCE MY PARENTS TO SEND ME TO GYMNASIUM, BUT MY MOTHER SAID THAT THERE WAS NO MONEY AND YELLED AT ME FOR PUTTING ON AIRS.

WHO DO YOU THINK YOU ARE?

ROTHSCHILD'S DAUGHTER?

* I both liked this and didn't. I was happy when I was near him, but I was also uncomfortable because everything I did seemed so clumsy.

I CRIED ALL NIGHT.

THE LEADERS OF PZ ASKED ME TO LEAD A TALK ON POLITICAL ECONOMY. I THREW MYSELF INTO THE TASK, READING EVERYWHERE. ONE DAY, WHEN I WAS SITTING IN THE SQUARE...

I LOOKED UP, AND THERE HE WAS.

MY HEART WAS POUNDING.

I COULD TELL HE WAS HAPPY TO SEE ME TOO.

* Anti-Zionist, Yiddishist, socialist party, devoted to an international brotherhood of workers and a nationalist Yiddish culture. Just to give you an idea of how seriously it took its mission, its full name was Algemeyner Yiddish Arbeiter Bund in Lite, Poylin un Rusland.

207

I HAVE NO POETIC IMAGINATION. FOR EVERYTHING UNEXPECTED I ALWAYS SAY THE SAME EXACT THING:

LIKE A THUNDERCLAP CAME THE NEWS.

THIS WHERE ONE REGISTERS TO JOIN POALEI ZION?

HG HAD BECOME A MEMBER OF PZ? HG HAD BECOME A MEMBER OF PZ! GOLDMAKHER OF ALL PEOPLE! SUCH A PRESTIGIOUS PERSON AMONG SUCH SIMPLE PEOPLE?

ALL DAY LONG I'D THINK ABOUT THE EVENING'S MEETING.

JOY FLOODED MY HEART.

NEVERTHELESS, EVEN THOUGH I HAD A STRONG CRAVING TO GO TO HIM, I DIDN'T. I DIDN'T WANT TO BETRAY WHAT WAS GOING ON IN MY HEART.

I THOUGHT THAT ONLY BY BEING COLDLY CONTROLLED WOULD I MAYBE DRAW HIM TO ME. I PRACTICED "GIRLISH DIPLOMACY." IT HURT, BUT THE PAIN WAS WELCOME. EVEN THOUGH IN MY HEART I KNEW HERSHL WOULD NEVER CHERISH ME, THAT MY DREAMS OF HIM WOULD NEVER COME TRUE.

AMAZINGLY, AT THE SAME TIME, MY DREAMS OF GOING TO GYMNASIUM BECAME REAL! THE LEADERS OF POALEI ZION HAD DECIDED TO HONOR ME.

THE PARTY HAS DECIDED TO RECOGNIZE YOU WITH A TEN-ZŁOTY-A-MONTH STIPEND FOR FURTHERING YOUR EDUCATION.

FURTHERMORE, WE HAVE ENGAGED AN INTERVIEW FOR YOU WITH THE DIRECTOR OF THE GYMNASIUM. REST ASSURED, OUR RECOMMENDATION WILL MEAN A LOT TO YOUR FUTURE PLANS.

I COULDN'T BELIEVE IT. IT SEEMED IMPOSSIBLE.* I WAS DRUNK WITH HAPPINESS, OUT OF THIS WORLD. I COULD ALMOST TASTE THE FRESH AND BEAUTIFUL LIFE THAT AWAITED ME.

ALL I COULD THINK ABOUT WAS ONE WORD.

Gymnasium *Gymnasium* *Gymnasium* *Gymnasium*

* I later learned that Hershl Goldmakher himself had secretly helped me out with some money. After all, he was one of the chosen ones, from a prestigious family, a good home, rich.

On my way to the interview I could only think about how romantic it all was, how I was like a hero in a book or a movie, struggling against overwhelming odds to reach her goal. I was determined to make a good impression. It seemed that even the strangers on the street were looking at me, admiring me, paying attention to me.

ENTER.

THE DIRECTOR WILL SEE YOU NOW.

PLEASE TAKE A SEAT.

I'VE BEEN TOLD THAT YOU DON'T KNOW A WORD OF HEBREW.

FORGIVE ME, YOUR HONOR.

DON'T BE ALARMED. JUST MASTER THIS MATERIAL. I HAVE IT ON GOOD AUTHORITY THAT SOME OF IT "MIGHT" BE ON THE ENTRANCE EXAM.

AND REMEMBER, DO PAY SPECIAL ATTENTION TO THE HEBREW.

ABOUT THE MONEY, HE DIDN'T MENTION A WORD, AND FROM THIS I DEDUCED HE WOULD ACCEPT THE TEN ZŁOTYS PZ HAD OFFERED.

212

NOW, LET ME SEE, OH YES, YOUR EXAM IS IN PRECISELY TEN DAYS' TIME.

I GATHERED MY VISIT WAS AT AN END.

AND HERE IT WAS THAT I COMMITTED A TERRIBLE ERROR. I TOTALLY FORGOT MYSELF.

I KISSED HIS HAND!

TODAY I CAN ONLY THINK THAT
I WAS SO SWEPT UP IN THE
ROMANTIC SCENES I'D READ ABOUT
THAT IT AFFECTED MY BEHAVIOR.

NOT REMEMBERING THAT I WAS
IN A PLACE WITH A CERTAIN
ETIQUETTE, I COMPLETELY
FORGOT MYSELF.

YOU HAVE TO UNDERSTAND THAT
FOR ME, GOING TO GYMNASIUM
WAS NOT A SIMPLE PAT THING, AS
IT WAS FOR OTHERS. THIS WAS
MY GREATEST DREAM, THE MOST
BEAUTIFUL DREAM, GOING BACK
YEARS AND YEARS.

WHEN I LEFT THE OFFICE I FELT AS IF I HAD COMMITTED A GREAT CRIME, AND I DIDN'T KNOW WHAT IT MEANT.

YET AS SOON AS I LEFT THE SCHOOL, I WENT TO MY SISTER'S AND WHEN I
DESCRIBED THE MEETING, I MADE IT SEEM GREAT. I COULDN'T HELP IT.

AND THEN THE DIRECTOR SAID, "YOU'VE
REALLY IMPRESSED ME, YOUNG LADY."

I STARTED SPENDING MORE TIME WITH
MY FRIENDS WHO WERE ALREADY
GOING TO GYMNASIUM. I FELT THAT
EVEN BEING ON MY WAY THERE RAISED
ME IN THEIR EYES. JUST SAYING THE
WORD "PROFESSORS" WAS A BIG
THING FOR ME. THEY EMBRACED ME AS
ONE OF THEIR OWN.

SWELL!

MAZEL TOV.

YOWZA!

EVEN RAKHELE M. INVITED ME OVER TO HER HOUSE! THIS WAS TRULY SOPHISTICATED, LIKE IN A FRED ASTAIRE MOVIE. A SPLENDID HOME WITH A HUGE YARD AND AN ARBOR. WE SAT THERE EATING CHERRIES FROM A BOWL. IT WAS LIKE SOMETHING IN A FAIRY TALE.

ON OUR WAY OUT, WE RAN INTO R'S MOTHER. SHE WAS COOL TO ME UNTIL RAKHELE MENTIONED I'D BE GOING TO GYMNASIUM IN THE COMING FALL. THEN THE MOTHER EXTENDED HER HAND TO ME.

MARVELOUS DARLING, SIMPLY MARVELOUS.

BUT WHEN I ARRIVED AT POALEI ZION FOR THE NEXT MEETING, I FELT SOMETHING WAS UP.

ENTER.

YOUR BEHAVIOR AT THE INTERVIEW WAS NOT GOOD. NOT GOOD AT ALL.

YOU UNDERSTAND THAT AS A SOCIALIST, YOU MUST NEVER* KOWTOW BY DOING SOMETHING LIKE KISSING THE DIRECTOR'S HAND.

SHANDA!

I THOUGHT I WOULD BURN UP FOR SHAME. I COULDN'T EVEN LIFT MY HEAD TO LOOK AT THEM. AND AT LAST I UNDERSTOOD WHY I'D FELT SO SAD AFTER MY VISIT TO THE DIRECTOR.

LIKE A SHE-DEVIL, THE TALK SETTLED OVER MY PLANS. EVEN THOUGH I WENT THROUGH THE MOTIONS, IN TRUTH I KNEW THAT BECAUSE OF WHAT HAPPENED, IT WAS ALL OVER.

* Or "need never," I don't remember exactly which he said.

EVEN MY LOVE FOR HERSHL GOLDMAKHER VANISHED.

AND, AT LAST, WHEN THE SCHOOL TERM BEGAN AND EVERYONE STARTED ASKING ME WHAT HAD HAPPENED AND WHY I WASN'T AT GYMNASIUM, AGAIN, I COULDN'T HELP MYSELF.

WHAT'S UP? YOU'VE MISSED THE WHOLE FIRST WEEK—

THE NEW MENU IN THE CAFETERIA IS TRULY HORRIBLE.

MY ZEYDE IN AMERICA, HE WAS GOING TO SEND ME THE MONEY.

BUT HE DIED.*

THE PITYING LOOKS EVERYONE GAVE ME HELPED RELIEVE MY PAIN.

BUT BEING IDLE WAS NO PLAN, SO I MOVED TO THE CITY.

NOW, EVERY DAY WHEN I PICK THE KIDS UP FROM SCHOOL, I KNOW I AM AT LEAST NURTURING A LITTLE GOODNESS IN THEM.

IF THEY SEE A POOR ORPHAN, THEY SHARE THEIR FOOD. NOT IN A SUPERIOR WAY, NO, THEY ARE COMPASSIONATE. THEY KNOW NOT TO LAUGH AT MENTAL ILLNESS.

* My grandfather was very much alive and he didn't live in America.

BUT TO BE COMPLETELY HONEST
(AS YOU HAVE INSISTED IN THE
RULES), THERE ARE MANY DAYS
WHEN I HATE THE CHILDREN.
WHEN I ONLY WANT TO BE RID
OF THEM, TO BE FREE.

WHICH IS WHY, AS I'VE SAID, EVERY FRIDAY I LOOK FORWARD TO MY EVENING OFF, WHEN I AM FREE TO RUN TO THE RINK AND SKATE.

BUT JUST LATELY, MY BEST FRIEND FROM HOME, LEAH, HAS STARTED TO SHOWER ME WITH LETTERS FROM GYMNASIUM SAYING, "I CAN'T LIVE WITHOUT YOU, I LONG FOR YOU."

SHE SAYS SHE SPOKE WITH HER FATHER ABOUT IT, AND TOLD HIM TO TELL THE DIRECTOR TO ACCEPT ME INTO THE SCHOOL FOR FREE. AND, LIKE A THUNDERCLAP, I JUST GOT A LETTER FROM HER SAYING HER FATHER HAS PROMISED HE WOULD DO EVERYTHING POSSIBLE, AND THAT HE BELIEVES THAT IF HE DOES, IT WILL ALL WORK OUT.

I THINK I'LL SIMPLY GO CRAZY WITH JOY.

THE AFTER

In early 2017, Jonathan Brent, the New York—based director of YIVO, got a surprising phone call and caught the next plane to Vilnius. Hundreds of documents had been uncovered in an abandoned church, and they were in Yiddish. The following flight from JFK brought Dr. David Fishman, chairman of the History Department at the Jewish Theological Seminary, who, when faced with the stacks of notebooks and ephemera, pronounced them "the most significant

finding in Jewish history since the Dead Sea Scrolls." And not long after that, **New York Times** readers were struck by a sepia-toned photo of a stern yet soulful young girl appearing under the headline "A Trove of Yiddish Artifacts Rescued from the Nazis, and Oblivion." The lost autobiographies had been found for the third time.

But that's not the end of the story. A **New York Times** editor picked up her phone to hear "The little girl in your article, that's my mother, her name was Beba Epstein." While most of the teenagers whose autobiographies were uncovered in Vilnius had perished at the hands of Nazis, it seemed that at least one had survived.

As soon as I heard about this, I knew I had to speak to that caller. And so, on a gray Sunday afternoon, seventy-nine years after the 150 zlotys prize for the Youth Autobiographies contest was supposed to have been awarded, I found myself on the phone with Michael Leventhal, the son of Beba "The Rule Breaker." One story he told me stayed with me. "For as long as any of us could remember," he said, "we celebrated Mom's birthday on December nineteenth. But as she got older, she began to insist her birthday was really the nineteenth of July."

Leventhal continued, "Even though Mom passed away a couple of years ago, when the article ran, a Yiddish-speaking friend of hers called me and said it was Beba's picture in the paper.

And sure enough, right there on the first page of her autobiography were the words "I was born in Vilna on July 19."

I felt the cold breeze of

seventy-nine years waft through the phone line.

A breeze that carried me all the way to Vilnius, where, four months later, I found myself in the briskly air-conditioned National Library turning the pages of one after another of the lost autobiographies.

In some sense, these were ordinary student notebooks. But each had details that made it seem to come alive. One, with delicate pages and tiny, precise letters in green between black, faux-leather covers. Another, with sloppy pencil scribbles scrawling outside the lines of a baby blue notebook, a map of Poland circa 1936 on its cover. Another, tight black lettering and intricate drawings, almost a graphic memoir.

And then I got it. What I was seeing, and feeling, weren't notebooks at all. They were voices, garments, smiles, tears, laughter—each one a distinct individual, a survivor rescued (in a sense) by his or her own words from the lost nation of Yiddishuania, a person.

The library closed. I would return first thing in the morning. As I walked back to my room, down the long avenue that had once been named for a saint, then a czar, then a Communist theorist, and then a saint again, I didn't hear the traffic.

Instead, I heard the voice of my own bubbe, my own grandmother speaking into the pink dial phone stuck to the kitchen wall in her Chicago apartment. I heard her whispering to her cousin or sister or brother in that strange backwards-sounding language to protect my young American ears from "things you shouldn't know about."

Protect them from what? From what had happened in Yiddishuania? From boys and girls pretty much my age with pretty much my same wants and fears and desires and dreams? Music. Rebellion. Courage. Sex.

The following morning, in Vilnius, I turned to the archivist as she handed me another notebook and I started to tell her about my phone call with Beba's son. I didn't get out more than a sentence or two when she stopped me. "Hold that thought," she said as she dashed off to her office and returned with a copy of David E. Fishman's **The Book Smugglers** in hand. She licked her forefinger (just like my bubbe always used to do when she read the paper) and turned to the footnotes at the end of the book. Running her finger down page 257, she landed on footnote 22 from chapter 5. And there was that name, again. Beba Epstein.

I took off my glasses and

peered at the small print. Turns out, prior to escaping the Vilna Ghetto and joining the Russian partisans, Beba herself had been a member of The Paper Brigade, risking her life to smuggle the archives of YIVO to safety. Her autobiography was part of the first wave of the competition and, in a reckless disregard for the rules, which specified applicants had to be at least thirteen, she submitted it when she was only eleven, in 1933. I quickly did the math and figured that, by 1943, it was as a twenty-one-year-old orphan (yes, her entire family perished) that Beba had joined with the poets, writers, artists, and thinkers who were defying the Gestapo to protect the treasures of Yiddishuania from Der Institut Zur Erforschung Der Judenfrage. Including, very possibly, and definitely without her knowing it, the very autobiography whose cover was pictured in the October 18, 2017, issue of the **New York Times**. HER story. She risked her life to save it, unaware of what she was doing. Never aware.

Or was she?

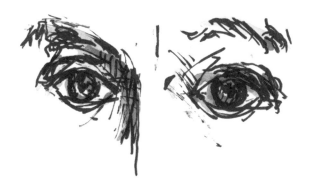

2009

Beba Epstein and her grandchildren Ariel and Noah

ACKNOWLEDGMENTS

Dozens of people have guided me on this journey to Yiddishuania, so many it is impossible to list (or very possibly remember) them all. First among equals, however, thanks must go to Ellen Cassedy, my intrepid, indefatigable and immensely talented translator, who squinted, searched, and solved the Yiddish scrawls of way more than the six autobiographies that made it into this book. I open my heart to Michael Leventhal, Beba Epstein's son, and to his family whose honesty, integrity, and passion ignited this project. I owe so much to the talented and enthusiastic professionals at the Martynas Mažvydas National Library of Lithuania, who welcomed me and my sketchbooks; Lara Lempert, Migle Anusauskaite, and Prof. Dr. Renaldas Gudauskas, director general. Literally and figuratively, this book owes its existence to YIVO, its director, Dr. Jonathan Brent, Dr. Alyssa Quint, Eddy Portnoy, and everyone sustaining Max Weinreich's vision. Thank you to Dr. David Fishman and to my editor and "lens" Nancy Miller; my agent and friend, Jennifer Lyons; my wife and muse, Alex Sinclair; my mother (and Litvish inspiration), Joan Krimstein; my kids (and toughest editors), Ruby, Noah, and Milo; my cousins, Michelle and Debbie Greenberg; and to . . . Peter Kuper, Joseph Berger, Faye Ran, Kai Bird, Anne Heller, Dr. Marcus Mosely, Lyudmila Sholokhova, Dr. Ilya Lempert, Barbara Harshav, Dr. Karen Underhill, Dr. Dan McAdams, Howard Reich, Dr. Marc Slutsky, Amy Schwartz, Rabbi Marc Belgrade, Rabbi Jeremy Kalmanofsky, Sam and Isabel Gross, Bob Eckstein, Michael Maslin, Ken Gertz, Bill Brichta, SallyAnne McCartin, Rosie Mahorter, Marie Coolman, Chris and the team at Quartet Printing in Evanston, Laura Phillips, Patti Ratchford, Barbara Yelin, that guy in Vilnius who ran the music store and shared the stories of his grandmother, and to James Atlas, whom I will miss.

SOME SOURCES AND SUGGESTIONS FOR FURTHER READING

Of course the ultimate source for this book were the teenager's autobiographies themselves. They are there, in the archives of YIVO in New York and at the National Library of Lithuania in Vilnius. Protected, cataloged, in acid-free envelopes and humidity- and light-controlled rooms. Safe. Beyond that, a wealth of books and articles and collections (online and on paper) informed my research, visual, verbal, experiential. I read far and wide: diaries, memoirs, biographies, and histories. I leavened that with fiction and cinema, all part of the creative vibrancy of Yiddishuania in Europe and as it resonated to its exurbs in North and South America. Books pretty much start (and end) with Lucy Dawidowicz, the late scholar who, as a college-aged New York City student, headed to Vilna and a position as a researcher at YIVO in 1939, and, thanks to her U.S. passport, was able to escape just in time. Her excellent memoir of that sojourn, **From That Place and Time**, launched my research; I even relied on the map of old Vilna printed on the inside cover as I propelled Vilnius myself. But Dawidowicz's books don't stop there; her collection **The Golden Tradition** is an invaluable source for all the tones and flavors of Yiddishuanian literature and journalism. Delicious. Finally, a posthumous collection of her essays and articles, **The Jewish Presence**, showed her reflecting on her reflections. I am greatly indebted to Jeffrey Shandler's **Awakening Lives:**

Autobiographies of Jewish Youth in Poland Before the Holocaust, the first place I turned when I learned of the biographies, a great overview of the contest with translations of some of the diaries discovered prior to the major findings in the St. George's Cathedral I traveled to Vilnius to explore.

I can't even begin to measure the inspiration and information I gained from David Fishman's **The Book Smugglers**, including the divine thread that linked Beba with YIVO's culture warriors, in a very real sense. A terrific reference for all things YIVO is **YIVO and the Making of Modern Jewish Culture** by Cecile Kuznitz. To get even deeper into the nuances of Litvak culture and the various political/religious upheavals, **Lithuanian Yeshivas of the Nineteenth Century** by Shaul Stampfer made sense of a mad, swirling world of mysticism, musar, politics, and shifting borders. For a window on the equally radical offshoots of Yiddishuanian civilization, **Radical Poetics and Secular Jewish Culture**, assembled by Stephen Paul Miller and Daniel Morris, stretched my understanding in new and unexpected dimensions. The comics/graphic narrative **Yiddishkeit** by Harvey Pekar and Paul Buhle was an info-packed delight. One book that really helped transport me was **A World Passed By**, a travel guide by Marvin Lowenthal of the Jewish sights in Europe for American Jews published in 1938(!), on the brink of the abyss, which presented an unseen window to that world.

For visual reference, in addition to my own sketches, I gained so much from the taste and curation of several books, notably *Yiddishland*, originally published in France by Gerard Silvain; *Image Before My Eyes*, compiled by Lucjan Dobroszycki and Barbara Kirshenblatt-Gimblett; Roman Vishniac's masterpiece *A Vanished World*; and verbally and visually in Yaffa Eliach's *There Once Was a World: A 900-Year Chronicle of the Shtetl of Eishyshok*. But "facts" are never enough; to further inhabit this world I turned to culture, custom, and curios, in no particular order (they're all great): *Jewish Magic and Superstition: A Study in Folk Religion* by Joshua Trachtenberg; *Houses that Talk: Everyday Life in Zydu Street in the 19th-20th Century up to 1940*, published in 2018 in Vilnius; *The People and the Books* by Adam Kirsch, which expertly places Yiddish writing in the greater arc of history; *Shtetl: A Creative Anthology of Jewish Life in Eastern Europe*, a kaleidoscopic collection of Yiddish literature edited by Joachim Neugroschel; as well as a deep and delicious dive into the novels and stories of I. B. Singer, Sholem Aleichem, Mendele Sforim, I. L. Peretz, Chaim Grade, Avram Sutskever, and a special shout out to *Vilna My Vilna: Stories* by Abraham Karpinowitz.

As to the vagaries and urgencies of memory, and forgetting, I treasured *The Wandering Jews* by Joseph Roth, *Witness: Lessons from Elie Wiesel's Classroom* by

Ariel Burger, and the very provocative and insightful *A Primer for Forgetting* by Lewis Hyde.

And then there were the articles! (Thank you, academia.com.) Some highlights include: *Social Science as a "Weapon of the Weak": Max Weinreich, the Yiddish Scientific Institute, and the Study of Culture, Personality, and Prejudice* by Leila Zenderland, *The Russian and Polish Existentialism as Mirrored by the "Jewish Problem"* by Svetlana Klimova, *The Evolution of the Exclusion of Jewish Women from Ritual Practices* by Yossi Quint, *Defying Authority in the Pale* by Elissa Bemporad, *Max Weinreich, Assimilation and the Social Politics of Jewish Nation-Building* by Kamil Kijek, *Jewish Identity in Interwar Europe* by Dan Michman, *The Legacy of the Kelm School of Musar* by Geoffrey Claussen, *"Yiddish Literature for the Masses"?* by Alyssa Quint, *Exploring Psychological Themes Through Life-Narrative Accounts* by Dan P. McAdams, *Hasidism, Mitnagdism, and Contemporary American Judaism* by Shaul Magid, and Antony Polonsky's *Fragile Co-existence, Tragic Acceptance: The Politics and History of East European Jews*. A special delight was diving deeply into Yiddish cinema and music of the interwar years, and I would heartily recommend everyone doing the same.